JAGUAR

· T · H · E ·

Enduring Legend

Text and photography by

NICKY WRIGHT

ACKNOWLEDGEMENTS

The author gratefully acknowledges the invaluable assistance provided by the following individuals and organizations throughout the preparation of this book:
Terry Larson; Stephanie Tullman; Jerry McGlothin; Dave Titterington, Olde Car Shop, Phoenix, Arizona; Eric Freeh; George E. Alleger; Craig K. Harris; Dr. Richard and Dianne Foster; Dave and Kathy Wathen; Thomas Barrett/Barrett-Jackson; Larry Nicklin; Mike Cook and C. Hight Flexman of Jaguar Cars, Inc.; Jaguar Journal, Leonia, New Jersey; *Autocar-Motor*, U.K.; Publications International *Collectible Automobile*; Bob Keeler; Roy and Barb Hathaway; Mike Mullan; Milland Place Hotel, Milland, Nr. Liphook, Hants, U.K.; Mr. and Mrs. Peter Brett and Staff, Milland Place Hotel; Don and Jenny Hartman; Fuji Films; Pentax Cameras. Very special thanks are due to Dr. Richard Foster and Jim, as well as Terry Larson and Jaguar Cars – without their help this book would not have been possible. And not forgetting the 1990 Jaguar XJ6 Vanden Plas, which performed so well for me while in Arizona.

DESIGNED BY DICK RICHARDSON
EDITED BY JOHN PHILLIPS

CLB 2375
© 1991 Colour Library Books Ltd., Godalming, Surrey, England
First published in the United States in 1992 by SMITHMARK Publishers, Inc., 112 Madison Avenue, New York, NY 10016
Printed and bound in Spain
All rights reserved
ISBN 0 8317 5127 4

SMITHMARK books are available for bulk purchase for sales promotion and premium use. For details write or telephone the Manager of Special Sales, SMITHMARK Publishers Inc., 112 Madison Avenue, New York, NY 10016. (212) 532-6600.

JAGUAR

· T · H · E ·

Enduring Legend

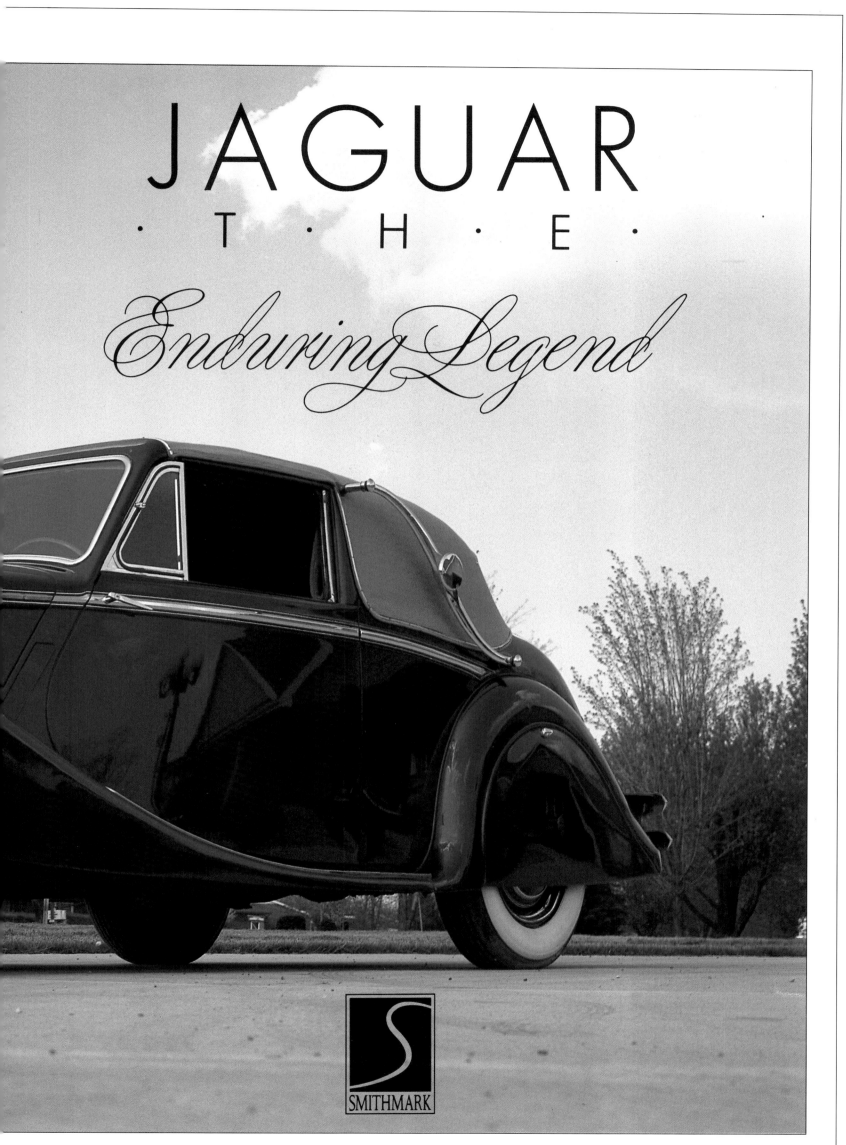

SMITHMARK

In memory of Richard Aspden, a nice man in a world that misunderstood.

fun making these cars. Beneath the grown-up exterior, there beat a small boy's heart whose dreams had come true.

Of course the creation of the first, the S.S., then the Jaguar, was more than just a small boy's fancy. If nothing else, Sir William was a hard businessman who also happened to be a talented romantic. A combination that is exceedingly rare. Either you're a good businessman and a lousy artist, or vice versa. But Sir William was both, which is perhaps why his cars have always appealed.

Facing page: the cockpit of one of Jaguar's greatest racing successes – the fabulous D-Type. The cars were driven with considerable success in many historic events by the likes of Mike Hawthorn, Paul Frere, Tony Rolt and Ken Wharton. Top: this identification symbol made many a heart beat faster ... especially if the owner of that heart happened to be behind the wheel of a V12 E-type. Top right: the famous Jaguar symbol, once an elegant hood ornament, is now just a badge due to today's safety requirements.

This book is about Jaguar. I refrain from calling it a history because space doesn't allow it to be, for even a concise history on this marque would run to several hundred pages because there is so much to tell. About the men who surrounded Sir William, who stayed with him for forty years or more. If that isn't loyalty, then what is? What I have tried to do is present a potted guide to this great British marque. I have not dwelled on Jaguar's later sporting activities because there is much to say and, again, no room to say it. Jaguar now has a fully fledged racing wing and its cars are tremendously successful, just as they were in the fifties. Even if not officially sponsored by the company, Jaguars have raced, mostly Mark IIs at Silverstone and Snetterton in the sixties. And winning – unless they came up against one of the big Ford Galaxies.

Jaguar is a fascinating story. A tale not of some faceless conglomerate that produces bland but pleasant automobiles, cars formed by computers and designers whom one never hears of. Read on and try to imagine yourselves, firstly at Blackpool, eventually at Browns Lane, Coventry. Study the freshly taken photographs (most of the cars herein were shot in America, a country infatuated with Jaguar) and imagine that you might have been one of those real people building real cars.

Heroes in fact.

CHAPTER ONE
THE BOYS FROM BLACKPOOL

Blackpool is a northern English seaside town noted for its fish and chips, large funfair and the brash flavor of its lifestyle. Brash is probably a description that would also fit the early Jaguars. Known as S.S. Cars before the war, Jaguar was the upstart of a relatively conservative British motor industry. High on style, rich in quality, Jaguar never failed to amaze. How the Blackpool-born company was able to build luxury cars at a fraction of the price of its rivals, echoes the American idiom; strong business sense allied with cost effectiveness.

Because Jaguars looked so much more expensive than they were, they were disparagingly referred to as "the poor man's Bentley" in well-to-do circles. Though rather petty, the term had a smattering of truth about it. Those who used to own Bentleys or Lagondas, but had fallen on hard times, could buy a Jaguar and keep up appearances. Likewise, those who never had money in the first place, but who wanted to impress the neighbors, they bought Jaguars.

Jaguar's founder, the late Sir William Lyons, was born in Blackpool in 1901, the son of respectable middle-class parents (his father owned a gramophone and piano repair business). He grew up in a comfortable environment near the sea and developed an interest in cars and motorcycles. Once he had left school, young Lyons got an apprentice job with Crossley Motors (long since defunct), but finding the work not to his liking he returned home and worked in his father's business for a time. Meanwhile, his enthusiasm for everything to do with motor cycles continued to grow.

William Lyons was barely 20 years old when he met William Walmsley, nine years his senior. What most attracted him was what Walmsley did; he reconditioned old motorcycles in a fairly large garage behind his house in Blackpool, and once the motorbike was finished, Walmsley added a stylish sidecar of his own design. He was quite happy to produce one a week; it gave him enough to live in reasonable comfort.

On 4th September 1922, the day of Lyons' 21st birthday, he and Walmsley formed the Swallow Sidecar Company on a 50-50 basis with assets of £1,000 (about $5,000 in those days) in the form of an overdraft from a sympathetic bank and guaranteed by the young men's respective fathers. In the months since Lyons met Walmsley, events had moved quite fast; even at this early stage of his motoring development, William Lyons displayed a tremendous talent for visual style, coupled with an excellent business head. To find a combination of the two in one person is rare indeed.

As is frequent in a partnership, one is retiring, more conservative, the other extrovert and brimming over with schemes for progress. This was Walmsley and Lyons; I need not tell you which one was the lad with the brashness of his hometown.

First Lyons restyled the motorcycle sidecars in the manner of an aircraft fuselage (but without wings and tail) and the sidecar wheel was a plain disc: no spokes, nothing. The sidecars were painted in numerous hues with wheels to match. By now Swallow Sidecars was established on the first and second floors of a small industrial building in Bloomfield Street, which was actually taken on before Lyons reached 21, again with the help of the fathers.

With the sidecars given the Buck Rogers treatment, Lyons started to advertise. Business was brisk and the fledgling company was able to fulfil orders because Lyons wisely took on additional labor to cope with what he knew would be a large demand. We should remember that in the early

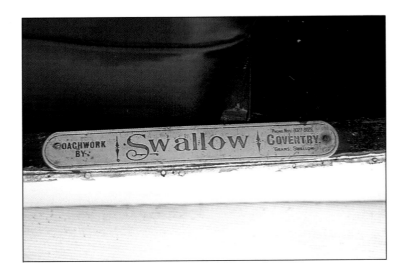

From humble beginnings as a manufacturer of motorcycle sidecars, Swallow Sidecars soon began customizing automobiles such as the popular Austin Seven, which they renamed the Austin Swallow (above). As can be seen from the plate (top), Swallow Sidecars had by now moved premises from Blackpool to Coventry, the heart of Britain's automobile industry. The example illustrated, with its tiny four-cylinder sidevalve engine (facing page bottom), is the only Austin Swallow known to be in the U.S. and belongs to Dr. Richard Foster of Newcastle, Indiana.

Facing page top: the Austin Swallow's vee'd windshield has an opening window on the driver's side. Calibration of the speedometer to 60 mph (facing page bottom) was optimistic in one of Britain's most popular runabouts, made even more appealing by the Swallow Sidecars treatment. As can be seen from the photograph (right), this car has yet to be restored. Note the wooden dash and wood cappings on the doors. The model illustrated is a saloon-bodied Swallow, which joined the original two-seater version in November 1928, barely a year after the introduction of the company's first car conversion.

1938 JAGUAR SS100

SPECIFICATION
1938 SS100

Engine: 2·5 litre 2663cc. Cylinder head: Weslake ohv in cast iron. Bore and stroke: 73 x 106mm. Max. power: 102bhp at 4600rpm. Max. torque: N/A. Compression ratio: 7:1. Carburetion: 2 x 1·5in. SU.

Chassis: Front suspension: beam axle, half-elliptic springs. Rear suspension: live axle, half-elliptic springs. Steering: — Brakes: Girling rod-operated, finned drums.

Measurements: Weight: 23cwt. Tires and wheels: 5·50 or 5·25 x 18in on 18in knock-off wire wheels. Track: front and rear 4ft 6in. Wheelbase: 8ft 8in. Overall length: 12ft 6in. Overall width: 5ft 3in. Overall height: 4ft 6in (to top of windscreen). Maximum speed: 94mph. Fuel consumption: 20mpg.

Another legendary car from Dr. Foster's Jaguar collection is this beautiful SS 100 (these and previous pages). Sleek and powerful, the SS 100 used a modified Standard six to propel it. Announced in 1935, the same year that the name Jaguar was adopted by the company, the SS 100 caused quite a stir in motoring circles. Originally equipped with a 2.5-liter engine, the 100 was in 1938 given a 3.5-liter unit that boosted the car's top speed to over 100 mph. The model illustrated boasts the larger engine (facing page top).

twenties there were few cars the ordinary man or woman in the street could afford, hence the popularity of the motorcycle and sidecar. The main threat to the promising motorcycle/sidecar business was Herbert Austin's little Austin Seven which, launched in 1922 at £165 ($825) and cheaper than either the ubiquitous Model T Ford (assembled in the U.K.) and the Morris Cowley, was truly cheap motoring

A stand became available at the 1923 Motorcycle Show and Lyons wasted no time in filling it. Assisting at the Swallow exhibit was a 17-year-old youth called Arthur Whittaker, who had recently joined the company. Whittaker went on to become buyer of parts and it is said he had an incredible knack of purchasing at bargain prices. He went on to become a director when S.S. Cars went public, and in 1961 Lyons made Whittaker Deputy Chairman, a position he held until his retirement, after 45 years service, in 1968.

By the mid-twenties – 1926 to be precise – Swallow Sidecars became the Swallow Sidecar & Coachbuilding Company and moved to larger premises in Cocker Street, Blackpool. This was to be S.S. & C.C.'s last home in Blackpool, but not before Lyons had ventured into building custom bodies for automobiles. Thus was born the Austin Swallow. Lyons had obtained an Austin Seven chassis and built a stylish two-seater body replete with a wasp tail and detachable top, the body being made of aluminum formed over an ash frame. Brightly painted and dashing enough to be the summer chariot in which the Oxford undergraduate could take his girl to the Henley Regatta or some such, the little "custom" car took off. Orders poured in, and what with sidecar sales still climbing, Swallow Sidecar & Coachbuilding Company was in a very healthy position after a mere five years.

Dealers clamored to get their hands on the Austin

Taillights (top) on the SS 100 bear a vague resemblance to the magnified head of a housefly. The SS emblem on the wheel locknut (top right) was innocent in 1938, but would have sinister connotations later on. Shock absorbers (above) were of a type in common use before the war, and the car was praised for its good handling and suspension. Typically British in appearance, this much-admired model was produced in very limited numbers until 1939, when manufacturing capacity was given over to the war effort.

Swallow, and soon Lyons had set up agreements with various dealers to distribute in certain areas of Britain. Henly's, for instance, was given sole rights to Southern England after placing an order for 500 Austin Swallows with Lyons. In 1928, after finding it was impossible to finish more than two cars a day, and that the cost of transporting materials was becoming a financial burden, Swallow Sidecars moved to Coventry, the heart of Britain's large motor industry and the area where most of Swallow's supplies originated. Once a thriving munitions factory during the First World War, grass now grew round the dilapidated factory that Swallow had acquired.

Prior to the move south, Swallow added two more models, one a sedan version of the Austin Swallow, the other a two-seater with rumble seat mounted on a Morris Cowley chassis. This had a four-cylinder engine double the size of the Austin (1550cc vs. 747cc) and was priced accordingly. One could buy an Austin Swallow for as little as £165, but the Morris Swallow cost £220. So few were made of the latter that it is almost sure to be an extinct species.

Once the old Coventry building had been prepared for full-scale production, Swallow began to churn out 50 custom-made sedans and two-seaters a week. Contrary to industry speculation, motorcycles still sold well and Swallow also had a full order book for sidecars. Like the Americans, Lyons saw that the fairer sex would soon be playing an increasing role in the purchase of automobiles, and to this end the luxuriously appointed Swallow saloon came with a lady's companion set.

Lyons, ever restless, looked around for other chassis to work with, and displayed on the Swallow stand at the 1929 Motor Show, a coachbuilt Swift Ten chassis and a Standard Big Nine. Although customized Swifts would be produced through 1931, it was the Standard connection that would shortly influence Swallow's fortunes to a great degree.

Production increased steadily to 100 cars a week, a commendable for a company building custom coachwork. Then came a turning point; the Standard Ensign with its 15-hp six-cylinder engine was given the Swallow treatment. Although only 50 were made, Lyons and Walmsley were much impressed by the engine, rated at 2054cc, and Swallow's days as a coachbuilder for other makers' chassis were numbered. Swallow Sidecars & Coachbuilding Company wanted to build its own car from the ground up, but with the exception of the engine. That would be left for Standard to supply its impressive six.

America's 1929 Wall Street crash had done its dirty work and spread its infection to Britain and Europe. Dole lines were becoming depressingly long and the situation remained difficult over a long period. But while some older, established car firms were feeling the pinch, the company

run by the boys from Blackpool kept on growing and selling, growing and selling.

For 1930 Lyons designed a very sporty body for the Wolseley Hornet chassis. The first to appear was a two seater complete with wire wheels and a waspish tail. Because the car was received so well, a four-seater model soon followed and both were produced until 1932. But in 1931 the public knew something special was going to be announced by Swallow, if the company's advertising was to be believed:

"Wait!" cried the advertisements in bold red letters. "The 'S.S.' is coming. S.S. is the new name of a new car that's going to thrill the hearts of the motoring public and the trade alike. It's something utterly new – different – better!" This advertising had the desired effect, and by the time the two S.S. models were unveiled at the 1931 London Motor Show, excitement was at fever pitch.

Standard Cars had contracted to supply Swallow with the 2054 six-cylinder engine and to design and produce a special chassis for the car that William Lyons envisaged. And what a vision! There was nothing like it, not even from the fashionable Italians – except that perhaps one could say the Alfa Romeo 1750 had a similar theme. Certainly the Corsica-bodied Daimler Double-Six one-off bore more than a passing resemblance; maybe this was prophetic, considering Jaguar would buy out Daimler thirty years later.

Like the handsome Cord L-29, the Ruxton, Alfa Romeo and Daimler Corsica, the striking new S.S. coupé was low. Very low. Its hood was longer than the rest of the car which had a high waistline, narrow side windows, a fabric covered roof and extremely wide rear quarters fitted with landau irons. A trunk with a top opening lid was fitted to the rear and carried an outside spare tire and wheel. The engine was the previously mentioned Standard side-valve six developing 16 hp. Top speed with this unit was about 70 mph and 0-50 (0-60 was unheard of in the thirties) took 20 seconds. Standard supplied an additional engine with a little more power, costing £10 more ($50), being a 2554cc

These and previous pages: the 1948 3.5-liter drophead coupé was a carryover from pre-war days, although for obvious reasons the letters "SS" were dropped. Even though the car was of a pre-war design, it still attracted admiration from all who saw it. The elegant tool-kit (top), fitted in the trunk lid, shows the attention to detail typical of Jaguar.

SPECIFICATION
1948 3·5 LITER DHC

Engine: 6 cylinder 3485cc. Bore and stroke: 82 x 110mm. Max. power: 125bhp at 4250rpm. Max. torque: 120lb/ft at 2000rpm. Compression ratio: 6·7:1. Carburetion: 2 x 1·5in. SU.
Chassis: Front suspension: independent, wishbone, torsion bar, anti-roll bar. Rear suspension: live axle, half-elliptic leaf. Steering: Burman recirculating ball. Brakes: Girling Hydraulic.
Measurements: Weight: 33cwt. Tires and wheels: 6·70 x 16in, bolt-on disc wheels. Track: front 4ft 8in, rear 4ft 8in. Wheelbase: 10ft. Overall length: 15ft 7in. Overall width: 5ft 8½in. Overall height: 5ft 2½in. Maximum speed: 91mph. Fuel consumption: 16-18mph.

Traditional wood and leather interior (facing page top) was a Jaguar trademark. The drophead coupé's 3.5-liter engine (facing page bottom) was an ohv six based on pre-war Standard design. A top speed of 91 mph gave this attractive car an edge over anything either side of the Atlantic, and helped establish the Jaguar name in the United States.

unit rated at 20 hp (55 bhp). This added about 5 mph to the maximum speed.

Priced at £310 and £320, depending on which engine the customer chose, the S.S. I was the hit of the year. Supplementing the S.S. I was the smaller S.S. II. The styling was the same as the S.S. I but came on the Standard Little Nine chassis with its four cylinder 1066cc engine as part of the package. At £210 the smaller S.S. was a remarkably well finished car for the price even if its top speed of 60 mph and 0-50 time of 26.6 seconds was nothing to write home about. Not for a car that looked so sporty, anyway.

Between 1931 and 1932 502 examples of the S.S. I were built; then (as Swallow advertising used to say) "The car with the 1000 look" was altered and refined in readiness for the 1932 Motor Show. Seven inches were added to the wheelbase, thus allowing the car to become a full four-seater. Due to the low chassis the seats were split by the drive shaft; not that this really mattered, for the car wasn't wide enough to accommodate a third passenger in the rear.

Horsepower was given a slight boost and both engines were increased in size for 1934. Now the smaller of the two

SPECIFICATION
1949 XK120 ROADSTER
(ALL ALUMINUM)

Engine: 6 cylinders, 3442cc. Twin ohc. Coil ignition. Clutch: SDP and final drive. Max. power: 160 at 5000rpm. Carburetion: 2 x SU horizontal.
Chassis: Front suspension: independent, wishbone, torsion bar, anti-roll bar. Rear suspension: live axle, semi-elliptic rear springs.
Measurements: Tires: 6·00 x 16 on 16 x 5K solid wheels.

Announced at the 1948 London Motor Show, the Jaguar XK120 sports car (these and previous pages) set the world alight. The first in a series of XK models, the formidable 120 was one of the fastest unsupercharged production cars in the world, with a top speed set conservatively at 120 mph and a 0-60 time of around 10 seconds. Developed under the direction of William Heynes, Jaguar's Chief Engineer, the magnificent DOHC engine (top) was a masterpiece of engineering. A batch of just two hundred of the aluminum-bodied cars was made before demand dictated that the company switch to pressed steel bodies.

had a cc rating of 2143, the larger was 2663cc. Acceleration and top speed were still disappointing. Nevertheless at least 1299 were produced from 1933 to 1936. Another model appeared in 1933, the S.S. I Tourer, and later in the year a sedan version was introduced. Basically the same as the coupé but with the addition of an extra window on each side, the sedan sold the most between 1933 and 1936. As for the S.S. II, it received the same treatment, and was made available in coupé, tourer and sedan styles. The 1006cc side-valve four was bored out to 1343cc and 1608cc but didn't get anywhere much more quickly than before. Standard engines were plodding engines: very reliable, go-forever engines – performance engines they were not.

The S.S. I Tourer sold 186 examples between 1934 and 1935; the coupé 154 from 1934 to 1936, and the sedan was far and away the best seller with 905 built over the same period. What puzzled everybody was how S.S. Cars managed to show the world that quality doesn't necessarily have to be expensive. Perhaps it had something to do with Arthur Whittaker's prowess at being able to buy at the right price. Whatever it was, it made Jaguar one of the most revered makes in the world.

In America in 1934 the Chrysler Corporation, amid much fanfare, launched the ill-starred Airflow. Years ahead of its time, the Airflow threw out all the old notions of car building and was designed with the help of a wind tunnel to obtain aerodynamic efficiency. Of course, numerous imitators appeared; Volvo, Peugeot, the Hillman Airstream, they were all lookalikes but without the advantages of wind-tunnel testing. Although William Lyons wasn't too keen, he allowed a parody of the aerodynamic principle to be built.

Launched in September 1934, the S.S. I Airline adopted traditional lines until the windshield. Then the roof curved,

the lines following a fastback design – though a turtle might be a better description. Or possibly the 1950 Standard Vanguard saloon. Americans not familiar with the great Vanguard – not the battleship, the car – might recall some of their early post-war Detroit built fastbacks to see what I mean.

For the throwaway price of £360 (multiply by five for the dollar equivalent) S.S. made 624 Airlines before it was withdrawn in 1936. Like most of the Jaguars of that period, few survive to this day. All of them were made of aluminum over wooden frames. As we all know, wood rots if not constantly taken care of, consequently Australians switched to all-steel American cars in the mid-thirties because Britain's wooden-framed cars were meal tickets for hordes of hungry termites.

An event that would set the seal on the company now known as Jaguar, took place in November 1934. William Walmsley resigned, the partnership dissolved. Always unwilling to follow his younger partner's ambitious schemes and not equipped to cope with the rapid expansion of S.S. Cars (as the company was then called), Walmsley felt it would be better to throw in the towel.

In January 1935 S.S. Cars Limited went public and William Lyons assumed the mantle of Chairman and Managing Director of the company. He was 33 years old and in charge of an incredible success story that had started in a little garage in his hometown thirteen years earlier. Two further models were introduced in March; the S.S. I drophead and the S.S. 90. The Drophead featured a folding top that disappeared from view under a hinged cover behind the seats.

Only twenty-four S.S. 90s were built during its brief life – it began and ended in 1935 – but the 90 was Lyons' first

1951 JAGUAR MARK V DROPHEAD COUPE

SPECIFICATION
1951 MARK V DHC

Engine: 2663cc. Cylinder head: cast iron. Valves and valve gear: overhead pushrod. Bore and stroke: 73 x 106mm. Max. power: 102bhp at 4600rpm. Compression ratio: 7·3:1. Carburetion: 2 x SU 1·375in.

Chassis: Front suspension: independent, wishbone, torsion bar, anti-roll bar. Rear suspension: live axle, half elliptics. Steering: Burman recirculating ball worm-and-nut. Brakes: Girling hydraulic (2LS front).

Measurements: Weight: 32·5cwt. Tires and wheels: Dunlop 6·70 x 16 covers on 5K x 16in bolt on pressed-steel wheels. Track: front 4ft 8in rear 4ft 9·5in. Wheelbase: 10ft. Overall length: 15ft 7in. Overall width: 5ft 9in. Overall height: 5ft 2·5in.

Jaguar's first post-war design, the Mark V (these and previous pages) was evolutionary rather than revolutionary. Much of the car clung to pre-war thinking but was handsome nonetheless. Landau iron (top left) and lamps (top right) were still very much pre-war, as were the interior fittings. Available both in saloon and drophead coupé form, the Mark V also came with the option of either 2.5 or 3.5-liter engine. A rear view (facing page) of this elegant car shows off its classic lines to advantage.

attempt at anything like a true sports car. Certainly exciting to look at, the S.S. 90 didn't deliver on performance, even though a well-known engineer, Harry Weslake, worked on the engine, which was Standard's 2663cc, 20 hp job. Perhaps a bit of an outcast in its day, the S.S. 90 is worth its weight in gold today. Before rushing off to scour the countryside, the chances of finding one are as remote as finding Tucker No. 52.

From 1935 S.S. automobiles would henceforth be known as S.S. Jaguar models, and the time had come for the company to have more of their own engineering designed in-house. William Lyons hired 32-year-old William Heynes, who came with a long list of recommendations, and appointed him Chief Engineer.

Though Lyons would probably never have admitted it, the hiring of Heynes was a stroke of genius that would catapult Jaguar to the forefront of motoring technology for years to come. From that moment on, almost everything that came from the Heynes-created engineering department bore the stamp of Heynes himself. It was he who designed new chassis, formulated the wonderful XK engine and much else.

New Jaguars came thick and fast from 1935 to the outbreak of the war. The Standard six cylinder engine was given more power by Harry Weslake, who converted it to overhead valve. This increased horsepower from 75 to 105 and a 2.5 liter sedan or tourer was capable of almost 90 mph. But the first Jaguar to hit 100 mph was the 3.5 liter version of one of the greatest Jaguars ever produced. When the general public saw the racy two seater alongside the tourers and sedans at the 1935 London Motor Show, they practically turned a cartwheel. Two models were displayed, one a 2.5, the other with the new 3.5 liter engine.

From rest to 50 mph took a mere 7.1 seconds, according to *Motor* magazine, who said the S.S. 100, as the car was named, " ... provides an exceptional performance through the gears" and later on, in the somewhat quaint English of the time: "The acceleration in top gear is so very rapid that the lazy driver may retain this ratio almost indefinitely."

Autocar was equally enthusiastic about the S.S. 100. Although the car had only a three-speed gearbox, the magazine said third was " ... a wonderful gear". And "a burst on this ratio for overtaking purposes sends the car shooting forward, and it is up into the 60 to 70 mph range extremely rapidly". The Girling brakes also came in for praise, as did the driving position: a word of caution was reserved for drivers over six feet, though.

No doubt about it, the S.S. 100 was a beautiful car. A thoroughbred even if it still relied on Standard power. Harry Weslake's modifications changed the whole character of the engine, putting the S.S. 100 way ahead of cheaper sports cars such as M.G., Riley Imp and Aero Minx and, surprisingly enough, ahead of several more expensive members of the breed. Standard continued to supply engines until the war and sold the tooling for the 2.5 and 3.5 to William Lyons in 1945.

By 1936 Jaguar had entered into competitive motoring. An S.S. 100 driven by Bill and Elsie Wisdom beat all-comers in the gruelling Alpine Trial, and class wins were posted at Shelsley Walsh and the Marne Sports Car Grand Prix at Rheims. Remember, this was only a 2.5 liter car; the 3.5 liter model was not introduced until the following year.

Despite the uncertainty of the times Jaguar sales were booming. So much so that William Lyons and his talented team realised there must be quicker ways of putting cars together than the traditional wooden frame overlaid with

steel panels. Why not do what the Americans had become so successful at doing? Construct the cars entirely out of steel. Not equipped to do the pressings, Jaguar turned to outside suppliers for its needs, but it was a decision Jaguar was soon to regret.

The troubled world of 1937 was troublesome also for Jaguar. The contracts for outside companies to supply manufactured steel parts for final assembly at the car factory resulted in a disastrous year – the supplies were frequently late in delivery, and occasionally did not arrive at all. Without essential parts production orders could not be fulfilled. Lyons, Whittaker and others made desperate visits to the suppliers, cajoling and threatening, until the troubles were solved. Some of the errant firms paid substantial compensation for the problems they had caused, and soon Jaguars were flowing out of the factory once more. If 1937 had been a bad year, 1938 saw record profits fill the company coffers even as the threat of war grew imminent.

The price of the 3.5 liter S.S. 100 was a more than modest £445. The cost of any S.S. Jaguar made the car an unbelievable bargain. The 1938 cars consisted of two-door convertibles, four-door sedans and the S.S. 100. Engine choices were 1.5, 2.5 and 3.5 liters. The 1.5 four cylinder was given Weslake's magic touch and was converted to overhead valve, thereby increasing horsepower and performance. A magnificent looking car with huge, heavily chromed headlights offset by the large Bentley style grille, a long hood augmented by a sweeping fender line, the 1.5-liter S.S. Jaguar didn't look out of place gracing the gravel driveways of a stately home. What was out of place was the extraordinary £298 to £318 price, the latter for the drophead. Only £415 bought the 2.5 liter drophead, while

SPECIFICATION
1952 MARK VII

Engine: 3442cc. Bore and stroke: 83 x 106mm. Max. power: 160bhp at 5200rpm. (150bhp at 5200rpm, 7:1). Compression ratio: 8:1 (7:1 optional). Carburetion: 2 x SU 1·75in H6.
Chassis: Front suspension: independent, wishbone, torsion bar, anti-roll bar. Rear suspension: live axle, half-elliptic leaf. Steering: Burman recirculating ball worm-and-nut. Brakes: Girling hydraulic servo assisted (two trailing shoe front).
Measurements: Weight: 34·5cwt. 53/47. Tires and wheels: Dunlop 6·70 x 16 covers on 16in 5K bolt on pressed-steel wheels. Track: front 4ft 8in rear 4ft 9·5in. Wheelbase: 10ft. Overall length: 16ft 4·5in. Overall width: 6ft 1in. Overall height: 5ft 3in. Maximum speed: 101mph. (102mph O/D). Fuel consumption: 17·6mpg.

the 3.5 liter drophead was priced at a staggering £465. The only cars that came close in price and comfort were the Buicks, Chryslers and Hudsons selling in increasing numbers in Britain. Where the Americans failed was in their overall standard of finish; compared to the Jaguars, they were non-starters.

There was further competition success for the S.S. 100s when they won the 1938 R.A.C. and Welsh rallies. Other events were entered with resounding success as Jaguar continued to confound the rest of the industry. One of the reasons that enabled Jaguar to produce cars at such low prices was rationalization. There were seven separate models, all sharing many components, and then there was Arthur Whittaker. Shrewder than an old-time barrow-boy, Whittaker had a knack of buying in components at price nobody else could achieve. Here then are two reasons why the cars could be produced for less than their rivals.

Sensing that war was coming, S.S. Cars phased out production of automobiles and turned instead to military contracts. Believe it or not, Swallow Coachbuilding Company was still producing sidecars; Lyons made that a separate company in 1935. Therefore the three military services were supplied with sidecars and trailers (the latter at a rate of 700 a week). The cars were put on the back burner while S.S. Cars settled down to concentrate on the war effort. In eighteen years the brash young man from the brash northern seaside town had come a long way. Shortly he would go further.

Jaguar's first true post-war design was swish, fat and a bit nouveau riche. A clever design aimed at the dollar market, the Mark VII (these and previous pages) remains as distinctive today as it was in 1950.

CHAPTER TWO
PARADISE TO PURGATORY AND BACK

During the war S.S. Cars concentrated on the manufacture of aircraft parts for Spitfires, Lancasters and others. As the tide turned and the enemy was finally routed, Sir John Black of Standard Cars informed Lyons that his company would be unable to supply 2.5 and 3.5 liter engines any longer. Once hostilities were over, Standard was pinning all its hopes on a series of small cars. Before Sir John could say more, Lyons made him an offer for the tools used to build the larger engines, and with the offer accepted S.S. had almost everything it needed under one roof.

Because the war left Britain almost bankrupt, the country faced a few years of deprivation and the need to rebuild. The government extolled industry to produce and export. Particularly to the United States, who, unlike its allies, emerged from the war more powerful than ever, with its countryside unscathed by destruction.

For companies like Jaguar Cars Ltd – the name was changed in the first months of 1945 because of the odious association the initials S.S. had acquired – the prospect of exporting to America was encouraging indeed. Like other

SPECIFICATION
1953 120C (C-TYPE)

Engine: 3442cc. Bore and stroke: 83 x 106mm. C-Type cylinder head. Max. power: 200bhp at 5800rpm. Max. torque: 220lb/ft at 3900rpm. Compression ratio: 8:1. Carburetion: 2 x 2in SU.
Chassis: Front suspension: independent wishbone, torsion bar, anti-roll bar. Rear suspension: torsion bars and rigid axle. Steering: – Brakes: Lockheed hydraulic drums.
Measurements: Weight: 20cwt. Tires and wheels: 6·00 x 16in front, 6·50 x 16in rear on 16in x 5K wire wheels. Track: front and rear 4ft 3in. Wheelbase: 8ft. Overall length: 13ft 1in. Overall width: 5ft 4·5in. Overall height: 3ft 6·5in. Maximum speed: 143·7mph. Fuel consumption: 16mpg.

Illustrated on these and previous pages is a replica of the famous XK120C, or C-Type racing car. Designed purely to win the Le Mans 24 hour race, the C-type was a competition development of the XK120 and Jaguar's first serious attempt at a racing car.

SPECIFICATION
1953 MARK VII SALOON

Engine: 3442cc. Bore and stroke: 83 x 106mm. Max. power: 160bhp at 5200rpm. (150bhp at 5200rpm, 7:1). Compression ratio: 8:1 (7:1 optional). Carburetion: 2 x SU 1·75in H6.

Chassis: Front suspension: independent, wishbone, torsion bar, anti-roll bar. Rear suspension: Live axle, half-elliptic leaf. Steering: Burman recirculating ball worm-and-nut. Brakes: Girling hydraulic servo assisted (two trailing shoe front).

Measurements: Weight: 34·5cwt. Tires and wheels: Dunlop 6·70 x 16 covers on 16in 5K bolt on pressed-steel wheels. Track: front 4ft 8in, rear 4ft 9·5in. Wheelbase: 10ft. Overall length: 16ft 4·5in. Overall width: 6ft 1in. Overall height: 5ft 3in. Maximum speed: 101mph. (102mph O/D). Fuel consumption: 17·6mpg.

Even if it was slightly vulgar, the Mark VII was a bargain hunter's dream. In England the car was priced at £1276 and offered a ride that many considered superior to that of a Rolls-Royce. With its polished wood and leather interior, luxury fittings and superb finish, the Mark VII rivalled cars costing many times its price. 12,755 rhd and 8184 lhd Mark VII models were made between 1951 and 1954.

Beautiful instrumentation set in an elegant wooden dash sets the tone for the Mark VII interior. Seating surfaces were all top quality leather. The car had nice detail touches, such as tool trays mounted in the front doors. Unusually large by British standards, the Mark VII had been designed with the lucrative American automobile market very much in mind.

car makers, Jaguar resumed production after the war with re-hashed pre-war models, albeit with modifications such as new shock absorbers, better brakes and the inclusion of an "air conditioning" system originally meant for the 1940 models. This was located at the firewall and was coupled to the engine water system. As well as providing interior heat, this rather basic unit also acted as a de-mister and windshield de-fogger.

As before, all three models shared many components, but there was a difference in wheelbase and overall length. The 1.5-liter car sat on a 112.8-inch wheelbase, had a 65.6-inch width and an overall length of 172.8 inches. Both the 2.5- and 3.5-liter cars were the same; 120-inch wheelbase, 66-inch width and 187.2 inches overall. As for the engines, Jaguar was able to build the bigger ones itself, but the 1.5 liter unit was still supplied by Standard.

American servicemen returning home from Britain and Europe had discovered quality cars built with interiors of polished walnut and Connolly hide upholstery. Compared to Chevrolets and Buicks, with their admittedly more serviceable, durable materials, these glossy, old-world vehicles spelled class. Then there were the sports cars. Those the G.I.s fell for in a big way. They had nothing like them in Baton Rouge! As each transport ship off-loaded thousands of troops, several M.G.s, Mercedes and other sports cars were unloaded too.

None of this escaped the notice of William Lyons. Already 35 per cent of Jaguar production was going overseas. A new sedan was in the works for 1949 but Jaguar was working on a high performance sports car to replace the S.S. 100 that had not resumed production after the war. Much of what Lyons wanted had already been discussed during factory fire-watching shifts, a necessary duty during the war just in case the plant was bombed. Lyons would converse with Heynes, Hassan and Bailey about new

engines, new models. Wallace Hassan had worked at Bentley and then got involved in the design of some racing specials, before joining Jaguar. Claude Bailey, who joined at the beginning of the war, succeeded Bill Heynes as Chief Engineer in 1945 when Heynes was appointed to the board of directors.

Even with Weslake's overhead valves, the Standard engines were becoming long in the tooth and certainly wouldn't be able to keep up with exotic new machinery soon to emerge from Italy. Jaguar engineers set to work on developing a modern, refined engine of 2.5 litres capable of putting out 160 bhp. Also considered was a four cylinder unit in the 1.5 liter range, and this would share much in common with the larger engine, thus allowing the same machinery to be used to produce both.

The designers built a 1360cc four-cylinder prototype engine which had hemispherical combustion chambers and dual overhead camshafts, the sort of design associated mostly with racing cars. But this was Jaguar, not Morris, not Ford; at Jaguar only the best was good enough – provided the price could be made right. Lyons liked the idea and suggested that work continue in this vein. More prototypes were built and each discarded because something wasn't quite right. Until finally the XK (all designs had X in their initials; this signified experimental) appeared.

If Chrysler thought it had the only hemispherical head, it was wrong. Jaguar's amazing new engine, introduced in the equally amazing XK 120 sports car at London's 1948 Motor Show, had an aluminum hemi-head and something Chrysler's V-8 didn't have – dual overhead camshafts. Cubic capacity of the DOHC six was 3442 and it was rated at 180 bhp.

As for the car, the XK 120 became an instant classic on sight; one look at the flowing lines took everyone's breath away. The designer of this superb automobile was William

The engine in the Mark VII was the same 3.5-liter DOHC unit as in the XK120, giving the big car a surprisingly nimble turn of speed and adding credence to the company's advertising slogan "Grace … Pace … Space." The Arizona license plate shows this particular Mark VII as having traveled a long way from its Coventry, England, birthplace.

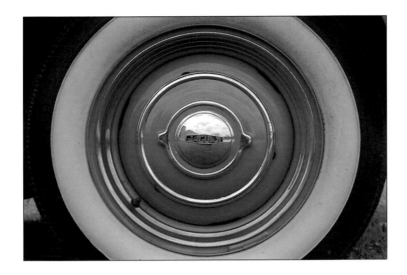

Lyons – he didn't delegate, he did things himself. It was one of those cars that can easily claim to be a work of art. From its fenders that sweep extravagantly into a dip at the rear of the door, up over the wheels and finishing in a softly rounded oval shape, the car made no bones that it was meant for speed. Other design features included the hood which flowed and narrowed into a semi-waterfall style grille between the large, flared headlights. The twin bumpers were decorative rather than practical, while the rear ones were non-existent save for what looked like a pair of bumper guards. The V-shaped windshield was the split variety and the roof line of the coupé was rounded, the thick rear pillars crescent shaped in profile.

Not only was the XK 120 an instant classic, it was an instant success too. Americans loved the car and orders came in thick and fast. It was such an attention getter it almost completely overshadowed the Mark V sedan introduced at the same time. Not a radical design like the XK 120, the Mark V was a great deal more traditional, even if the body was all new. It had long, sweeping front fenders that flowed into the rear. Options included deep rear-fender skirts.

Looking at this car, which shared the same crescent-shaped rear pillar design as the XK 120, the fine detail work becomes immediately apparent. Even though the price was £1,189 ($4161 – the pound was considerably devalued after the war) its looks and finish suggested at least double. As the new DOHC engine was to be used in a new series of Jaguar full-size sedans and dropheads being prepared for model year 1951, the Mark V was a car without a future, a transitional car that would be in production for only one year. So it was offered with the old diehard 2.5- and 3.5-liter engines once owned by Standard. What was new, however, was all independent front suspension, featuring torsion bars – sorry, Chrysler. Pipped again!

It is doubtful if even William Lyons realized the impact the XK 120 was going to make. Would you believe the intention was a limited run of 200 cars? Decked out in all-aluminum bodies, the XK 120 was supposed to be a tool to promote the new engine which, as we already know, would

On April 1, 1953 Jaguar announced the XK120 Drophead Coupé ... or convertible. This was the third model, the others, announced in 1949 and 1951, being the Open Roadster and Fixed Head Coupé. Whatever angle it is viewed from, this legendary model is a true thoroughbred.

soon see service in a new range of sedans. It wasn't long before the initial 200 had sold out, and with orders pouring in Jaguar quickly decided to continue production of the XK, but using steel bodies instead. At the time there was nothing else to touch it in terms of over-the-road performance. With a top speed of over 120 mph, the XK 120 was the fastest production car in the world.

The first XK 120 was a roadster and the fixed head coupé, mentioned above, didn't appear until 1951. Door cappings and dashboard were manufactured from walnut; overall the fixed head was more luxurious than the roadster. Nearly all XK 120 production was heading across the Atlantic, many of them ending up in the hands of movie celebrities who found the car's undeniably glamorous appeal quite on a par with their own.

In the year of the Festival of Britain, 1951, the company couldn't get enough cars across the Atlantic to fulfil the demand. And Jaguar entered the classic Le Mans 24 Hour race and won, the first British car to do so since 1935!

Prepared XK 120s had proved to the world since 1949 that they were capable of racing in competition. Three race-prepared XKs were given to drivers to run in a sports-car race organized at Silverstone in August 1949. The XKs were conspicuous by their success; it would have been a 1-2-3 sweep had one of the cars not blown a tire. A young driver named Stirling Moss won the 1950 Tourist Trophy race and Ian Appleyard won the 3-liter class in the Alpine Rally, while a youthful American, Phil Hill, took an XK to first place in the Californian Pebble Beach Cup Race.

Jaguars had entered Le Mans in 1950 and, racing an almost stock aluminum XK, driver Leslie Johnson was catching the leader when he was forced out after 21 hours. Two other entries finished 12th and 15th respectively. But in 1951 Jaguar came home first overall in what was then called the XK 120C, but better known today as the C-Type.

Like all good men who know their stuff, William Lyons

SPECIFICATION
1953 XK120

Engine: 3442cc. Bore and stroke: 83 x 106mm. Max. power: standard 190bhp at 5500rpm; special equipment 210bhp at 5750rpm. Max. torque: standard 210lb/ft at 2500rpm; special equipment 213lb/ft at 4000rpm. Compression ratio: 8:1. (7:1, 9:1 optional). Carburetion: 2 x 1¾in SU.

Chassis: Front suspension: independent wishbone, torsion bar, anti-roll bar. Rear suspension: live axle, semi-elliptic leaf springs. Brakes: Lockheed hydraulic drum, two leading shoe front, leading and trailing rear.

Measurements: Weight: 27·5cwt. Tires and wheels: 6·00 x 16in. Track: front 4ft 3in, rear 4ft 2in. Wheelbase: 8ft 6in. Overall length: 14ft 5in. Overall width: 5ft 1·5in. Overall height: — Maximum speed: 119·5mph. Fuel consumption: 14·5mpg.

The interior (facing page top) of the XK120 Drophead Coupé was taken from the Fixed Head and offered greater luxury than that of the Roadster. Headlamp design (facing page bottom left) is sensual and beautifully blended into the fenders. The grille (facing page bottom right) was expensive to produce and was changed to a cast unit with fewer strips on the 1955 XK140.

63

SPECIFICATION
1954 XK120 ROADSTER

Engine: 3442cc. Cylinder head: 'A' type alloy twin ohc. Bore and stroke: 83 x 106mm. Max. power: standard 160bhp at 5000rpm; special equipment 180bhp at 5300rpm. Max. tprque: standard 195lb/ft at 2500rpm; special equipment 203lb/ft at 4000rpm. Compression ratio: 8:1. (7:1 or 9:1 optional). Carburetion: 2 x 1·75in SU.
Chassis: Front suspension: independent wishbone, torsion bar, anti-roll bar. Rear suspension: live axle, semi-elliptic leaf springs. Brakes: drum, Lockheed hydraulic, two leading shoe front, leading and trailing rear.
Measurements: Weight: alloy car 25·5cwt; Steel car 26cwt. Tires and wheels: 6·00 x 16in on 16in x 5K solid wheels (later 5·5K); 16in x 5K wire wheels optional from March 1951, chromium plated wire wheels optional from 1953. Track: front 4ft 3in, rear 4ft 2in. Wheelbase: 8ft 6in. Overall length: 14ft 6in. Overall width: 5ft 1·5in. Overall height: 4ft 4·5in. Maximum speed: 124·6mph. Fuel consumption: 19·8mpg.

The Roadster (these and previous pages) was the first of the three XK120 variants, its aluminum body mounted on an ash frame. With demand outstripping all expectations, however, the company was obliged to tool up for "mass" production. The car shown is a 1954 model, fitted with wind wings (top).

1954 JAGUAR XK120 ROADSTER

Dashboard instruments (top) are traditional white on black; note that the rev counter goes anti-clockwise. The Jaguar's DOHC six (left) is one of the great engines of our time, and in 1949 it earned the XK120 recognition as the fastest production car on earth. Wire wheels (above) reflect the sporty nature of the car, but whitewall tires do not.

realized that racing improves the breed. He viewed the mixed fortunes of the nearly stock XK 120 racers with great interest and decided Jaguar had to build a proper competition sports car if it was to compete with that new-fangled Ferrari from Italy. So the C-Type was born, and made its first appearance at the 1951 Le Mans Race, which, as has already been mentioned, it won. Indeed, the C-Type won the race at the record speed of 93.49 mph, while another C-Type broke the lap record with a speed of 105.24 mph.

Even if the car was originally referred to as the XK 120C, this was a bit of a misnomer. Apart from the engine, which was the DOHC six rated at either 200 or 210 bhp and the transmission, everything else about the car was completely different. The chassis frame was a welded structure of tubes which gave greater torsional strength, and the suspension was independent up front with torsion bars while the rear eschewed the normal semi-elliptics for torsion bars. This arrangement worked well because the rear axle was located in such a manner as to supply improved adhesion without recourse to the de Dion system and universally jointed driveshafts.

The C-Type body was all aluminum and was made up of three sections attached to the frame by a series of bolts. Should access to the frame, suspension, engine and transmission be required, the whole body could be removed in a matter of minutes, even faster by a skilled racing-pit team. Engine accessibility under normal conditions was good. The entire front end hinged forward in much the same way as the E-Type of a few years later. Braking was supplied by Lockheed self-adjusting hydraulics drums. Top speed was a very fast 144 mph while 0-60 was achieved in 8.1 seconds.

Eleven C-Type works cars were built between 1951-53 while a further forty-three were production cars sold for £2,327 each between 1952-53. The so-called production versions were really built for club drivers to compete in, especially in America. Jaguar's own cars were managed by one "Lofty" England – "Lofty" because he was extremely tall. He masterminded Jaguar's racing fortunes, having joined the Coventry based company shortly after the war as Service Manager. Lofty had spent most of his motoring life on the racing side, and had worked with some of Britain's great drivers. Thus he was a natural to take over as Jaguar Team manager when the company decided to go racing.

It goes without saying that the XK 120C was an exciting car, but Jaguar had also launched its new range of Mark VII sedans. Announced at the 1950 Earls Court Motor Show in London, the Mark VII was an immediate hit on both sides of the Atlantic, especially in America, where its very large size and width suited American tastes well. To many Englishmen the Mark VII was "Blackpool Brash" (my choice of words) the sort of car the *nouveau riche* might buy. Mind you, the VII was a magnificent vehicle blessed with interior fittings of walnut veneer and top leather upholstery. Very quiet, outrageously comfortable, the Mark VII might have been described as decadent by some. As it was, *Autocar* said in its first paragraph that " … in performance and in road behavior, as in appearance and finish, this is one of the most impressive cars available in the world today." This excerpt from *Autocar's* February 1952 issue was from a road test conducted in Europe and England over six months. The car was also entered in the Monte Carlo Rally.

In those days, *Autocar* tended to give high praise to anything that came out of a British factory, reserving criticisms for foreign cars only. Perhaps it helped the export drive, but I rather think the testers' enthusiasm got a little out of hand when they claimed they " … travelled all the way from the Riviera to the Channel coast … and happily

SPECIFICATION
1955 D TYPE RACER

Engine: 3442cc. Cylinder head: 'Production D Type' (c-type casting, but 1⅞in inlet valves, gas flowed etc. Valve angle 35/35). Bore and stroke: 83 x 106mm. Max. power: 250bhp at 5750rpm. Max. torque: 242lb/ft at 4000/4500rpm. Compression ratio: 9:1. Carburetion: 3 x Weber DCO 3/45mm.
Chassis: Front suspension: independent wishbone, torsion bar. Rear suspension: live axle, trailing links, transverse torsion bar. Brakes: Dunlop discs, triple pad front, twin pad rear.
Measurements: Weight: 17cwt (dry). Tires and wheels: Dunlop Racing 6·5 x 16in, on 16in x 5·5K. Dunlop light alloy centre-lock wheels. Similar wheels but of 17in diameter could be obtained. Track: front 4ft 2in, rear 4ft 0in. Wheelbase: 7ft 6⅝in. Overall length: 12ft 10in. Overall width: 5ft 5⅜in. Overall height: 2ft 7·5in. (at scuttle). Maximum speed: 162mph. Fuel consumption: 9 – 14mpg.

These and previous pages: this particular D-Type has something of a pedigree: it was raced at Le Mans in 1957 and came in third overall. 1957 was a memorable year for Jaguar as their cars took the first three places at the world-famous 24-hour endurance race. Not only a good road engine but a successful racing one as well, Jaguar's DOHC 3.5-liter six was capable of over 140 mph in competition trim.

maintained speeds of up to 80 mph on treacherous and slippery roads ...." According to this report snow was thick on the ground in some areas.

At 197 inches overall, the Mark VII was a big car indeed, as big as many American cars of the period. Although the interior very definitely smacked of British tradition it had a very transatlantic flavor. Not according to Motor magazine's report: "The Jaguar is essentially a European as distinct from an American product ...." Having got that off their chests the testers had to admit the car was obviously aimed to please the American consumer. I don't think *Motor* cared very much for the overall design. "In the future there will be better cars than the Mark VII, for the art and science of car design remain far short of finality," was *Motor's* opinion. In other words, they were not too happy with the Mark VII and this was a delicate way of putting it without ruffling too many feathers.

By 1953 money was flowing into Britain's coffers again, the rebuilding of bombed-out cities was almost complete, and rationing and shortages had almost disappeared. The motor industry, relaxed in the knowledge that they had a large export market, now started to aim their products at domestic customers who were only too eager to buy.

Even though money had been devalued, the Jaguar was still a remarkable bargain and there was nothing to touch it. At £1,693 the Mark VII Jaguar represented a "best buy" whichever way one looked at it. Actually the car's true price was only £1,088 – the extra £606 was a form of sales tax introduced during the war. Purchase tax – as it was called – didn't stop nearly 13,000 Mark VII sedans finding British homes between 1951 and 1954, while a further 8,184 went abroad, mostly to America.

Many Americans prefer the convenience of an automatic transmission and this was not lost on Jaguar, who offered a Borg-Warner unit on the Mark VII early in

1955 JAGUAR D TYPE RACER

1953. The torque-converter type transmission was similar to the one used by Studebaker but the shift lever was rather small and set in the dashboard, ahead of the driver. Shifting was smooth and positive with brisk acceleration provided by the normal kick-down on the throttle. This transmission was only available on Jaguars going to America; it was not offered on domestic models until much later.

Mark VII Jaguars did well for themselves in competition; in the new Production Touring Race at Silverstone in May 1952, Stirling Moss drove one to an impressive victory. Another Mark VII was second in the Tulip Rally. In 1953 Ian Appleyard finished first in the Tulip Rally and Stirling Moss repeated his Silverstone success of the year before. And so it went on, in whatever event a Jaguar was sure to be in the top five places, with the exception of Formula One racing which the company left alone. I think Lyons probably felt that it was far better to compete in sports-car racing with cars that had at least some resemblance to those sold by Jaguar dealers. Nobody in their wildest dreams could claim a Formula One racing car looked anything like road-going machinery.

A modified Mark VII, the Mark VIIM, was introduced in 1954. It had a much more sporting flavor and was powered by the XK 140's close-ratio four-speed box, and its stiffer suspension improved the already good ride. Priced at £1,616, the Mark VIIM saw production of 10,061 units between 1954 and 1957. One change was the removal of the archaic semaphore indicators which were replaced by the flashing type of turn signals.

June 1954. Spectators craned their necks to see what the new car was at the starting grid. The 1954 24 Hour Race at Le Mans was about to begin. There were no Jaguar C-Types. Ferrari, Alfa-Romeo, Talbot and Mercedes, yes. And a formidable looking vehicle with a shark-like fin at the rear. This was Jaguar's new D-Type, soon to become on of the world's sporting legends.

Knock-off hubs (top) were designed for quick wheel changes. The shark fin (right) was a trademark of D-Types – an addition that improved the stability at speed of these classic machines. In 1958 driver Jean Marie (Mary) Brussin was killed in this car when he spun out of control under the Dunlop Bridge during the Le Mans race. The car was eventually restored using the original components.

74

After the XK120 came the virtually identical XK140, followed in May 1957 by the XK150 (these and previous pages). Fatter, slab-sided and more luxurious, the XK150 was more a tourer than an out-and-out sportscar. A one-piece curved windshield was now fitted on both available body styles, and the Roadster variant was no more. Massive bumpers were similar to those of the XK140, and had been designed with the American market very much in mind. The transatlantic influence was also visible in the design of the dashboard (top).

CHAPTER THREE
GRACE, SPACE, PACE

Jaguar's racing successes had made the go-ahead Coventry company a household word. Any car that wins Le Mans is a car to be reckoned with; it has to be good. A lone C-Type crossed the finishing line in 1951 as winner of this most legendary race and Jaguar hoped for more or the same in 1952. A team of three works C-Types were fitted with longer, lower bodies more streamlined than before. Unfortunately, not enough time was available for thorough testing, and as a result all three cars overheated due to insufficient cooling, retiring early in the race, their engines destroyed.

Jaguar had been having talks with Dunlop about acquiring its new disc brakes to try on the C-Types. Should they prove satisfactory, then why not fit production cars with the same? Naturally Dunlop was more than interested in the proposal and eagerly agreed.

About the same time, millionaire sportsman Briggs Cunningham, builder of the great Chrysler-powered Cunningham roadsters, had been negotiating with Dunlop to supply him with disc brakes for his cars. Dunlop agreed this would be possible and Cunningham was secure in the knowledge that his cars could win Le Mans with ease, if fitted with disc brakes. In the three Le Mans in which he had entered his own cars, Briggs Cunningham felt it was the brakes that had let his team down, not the engines. The Chrysler hemis were big enough and powerful enough to blaze a trail to the moon and back – if they had the stopping power. As Briggs was to say much later, he felt he had been cheated. At the last minute Dunlop refused to allow him to have its disc brakes because of the deal with Jaguar. After all, Jaguar was holding out a tempting carrot

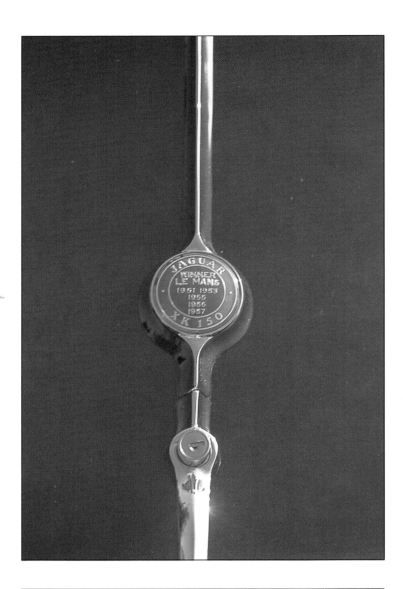

SPECIFICATION
1959 XK150 FHC

Engine: 3442cc. Cylinder head uprated 'A' type standard; 'C' Type special equipment. Bore and stroke: 83 x 106mm. Max. power: standard 190bhp at 5500rpm; special equipment 210bhp at 5500rpm. Max. torque: standard 210lb/ft at 2500rpm; special equipment 216lb/ft at 3000rpm. Compression ratio: 8:1 (7:1 and 9:1 optional). Carburetion: 2 x 1¾in. SU.
Chassis: Front suspension: independent wishbones, torsion bars, anti-roll bar. Rear suspension: live axle, semi-elliptic leaf springs.
Measurements: Weight: 28·75cwt. (DHC, add 300lb). Tires and wheels: 6·00 x 16in on 16in x 5K wire wheels, or 16in x 5·5K solid wheels (basic models). Track: front and rear 4ft 3·25in. Wheelbase: 8ft 6in. Overall length: 14ft 9in. Overall width: 5ft 4·5in. Overall height: 4ft 7in. Maximum speed: 123·7mph. Fuel consumption: 20·5mpg.

Few manufacturers could boast Jaguar's racing pedigree, and the distinctive trunk badge (top) proudly records Jaguar's five Le Mans wins. The company had pulled out of racing in 1956, although private entrants, notably Ecurie Ecosse in 1957, continued to run Jaguars in competition. Despite its acknowledged good looks and still very respectable performance, the XK150 was now showing signs of ageing.

SPECIFICATION
1960 MARK IX SALOON

Engine: 3781cc. Cylinder head: 'B-type' aluminum alloy, hemispherical combustion chambers. Bore and stroke: 87 x 106mm. Max. power: 220bhp at 5500rpm. Max. torque: 240lb/ft at 3000rpm. Compression ratio: 8:1 (7:1 optional). Carburetion: 2 x SU 1·75 HD6.
Chassis: As for Mark VIII except: Steering: Burman recirculating ball worm-and-nut, power assisted. Brakes: Dunlop disc, 12·125in. dia. front, 12in dia. rear, servo assisted.
Measurements: Weight: 35·5cwt. Maximum speed: 114·3mph. Fuel consumption: 13·5mpg.

A combination of American convenience and British tradition greeted the buyer of the new Mark IX saloon (these and previous pages), introduced in October 1958. As can be seen, the Mark IX interior (facing page top) was a mixture of leather and walnut. Lithe Jaguar emblem (facing page bottom) crowns the car with grace. While Chrysler boasted about its torsion bars in 1957, Jaguar had them on Mark VIIs in 1952. The Mark IX had torsion bars, disc brakes, and four-speed manual or Borg-Warner automatic transmission.

in the form of a possible contract for disc brakes on its production cars. Probably, according to Cunningham, Jaguar got wind of Dunlop's talks with the Californian-based millionaire and threatened to cancel any further discussions regarding the production cars. Dunlop was caught between the devil and the deep blue sea. Obviously the company's future would be at stake so they were forced to renege on Cunningham's request.

The Jaguars equipped with disc brakes drove a beautiful race. Besides the brakes, other modifications included a lightened body, three twin choke carburetors and a stiffer rear suspension. But it was the brakes that really clinched the race for Jaguar, who finished one, two and four. Tony Rolt and Duncan Hamilton drove the winning car, Stirling Moss and Robb Walker the second place Jaguar and preventing a clean sweep, a Cunningham, driven by Fitch and Walters, took a splendid third place. Fourth place was taken by Whitehead and Stewart in a C-Type. Although it was a terrific victory, it must have been galling not to have crossed the finishing line 1, 2, 3.

At least Briggs Cunningham had the satisfaction of knowing it was his car that prevented it. Poetic justice, perhaps, but the Cunningham ran a tremendous race, brakes notwithstanding. Nobody else had disc brakes either, so it is a matter of conjecture whether the Cunninghams could have won had they been so equipped. Can you imagine how the Ferraris might have done? Chances are that with disc brakes the Cunninghams would have won, for their huge and reliable Chrysler V-8s had proved willing workhorses with the capability for running mile after mile flat out, with never a splutter or whimper. Any weight disadvantages the Cunninghams might have had was balanced by the engine's power. Yes, there was definitely more than an outside possibility that Cunningham would

SPECIFICATION
1963 MARK X SALOON
3·8 LITER

Engine: 3781cc. Cylinder head: 'straight port', aluminum alloy, hemispherical combustion chambers. Bore and stroke: 87 x 106mm. Max. power: 265bhp at 5500rpm. Max. torque: 260lb/ft at 4000rpm. Compression ratio: 8:1 (7:1, 9:1 optional). Carburetion: 3 x SU 2in HD8.

Chassis: Steering: Burman recirculating ball, power assistance standard. Brakes: Dunlop discs, 10·75in front, 10in rear, Kelsey Hayes vacuum servo.

Measurements: Weight: 37cwt 1qr. Tires and wheels: Dunlop 7·5 x 14 RS5 covers on 5·5K x 14in bolt-on pressed-steel wheels. Track: front and rear 4ft 10in. Wheelbase: 10ft 0in. Overall length: 16ft 10in. Overall width: 6ft 4in. Overall height: 4ft 6·75in. Maximum speed: 119·5mph. Fuel consumption: 13·6mpg (14·1mpg).

The star of the 1961 London Motor Show was the striking Mark X (these and previous pages). The first large Jaguar to employ unitary construction, the Mark X was longer, lower and wider than ever before. Independent rear suspension and a 3.8-liter version of the tried and true DOHC six gave the car good manners and a top speed of 120 mph, despite its weight of 4144 lb. Interior appointments spoiled occupants with a profusion of walnut and leather.

have been the first American to win this exotic race twelve years before Ford swept across the finish line, 1, 2 and 3.

If the C-Type was good, the D-Type was even better. Very aerodynamic in shape the D-Type has achieved distinction as *the* sportscar of all time. And not without good reason, for its design was the forerunner of the legendary XK E-Type then still several years away. It also won a number of thrilling races, mostly in the capable hands of the Scottish racing team, Ecurie Ecosse.

Aerodynamics were Malcolm Sayer's forte, wind tunnels his argument for efficiently designed cars. After a stint with the Bristol Airplane Company, he was offered a job by Bill Heynes and joined Jaguar in 1950, where he put his aerodynamic theories to work, resulting in the C-Type. Sayer's design made good use of the wind tunnel and the C-Type was a blend of attractive styling and wind-cheating curves. These curves certainly helped to achieve two wins at Le Mans and with speeds approaching 150 mph down the straights, catching it wasn't easy.

One car that would surpass the C-Type was Sayer's D-Type. Once again Sayer designed the car in the wind tunnel and improvements included the plexiglass wrap-around windshield and streamlined headrest. To assist high speed stability at events like Le Mans, Sayer added the famous fin to the headrest. Like the C-Type, the front end lifted forward to expose engine, suspension and wheels, a feature the later E-Type would adopt. Again, like the C-Type, the D's rear bodywork was removable.

The D-Type was a monocoque construction, the central section formed out of magnesium alloy, and having double-skinned front and rear bulkheads. A tubular sub-frame carried the engine and front suspension, the latter consisting of double wishbones and torsion bars like the C-Type. The 3442cc DOHC six was much as before, with the exception of an increase in horsepower to 250. Tests showed the D-

Type was fast – very, very fast. Zero to sixty was accomplished in a mind-blowing 4.7 seconds, almost twice as fast as the C-Type, and maximum speed was over 162 mph for the "production" version, well over 170 mph for works cars.

Prepared in time for the 1954 Le Mans (this race was virtually the sole reason for first the C, then the D's existence), Jaguar's team, led by "Lofty" England, entered three D-Types. The opposition was formidable; Ferraris with 4.9 liter V-12s, Alfa-Romeos and a new threat, the Mercedes 300SLR. Hopes were high that the D-Types would repeat the success of the C-Types in 1953. Unfortunately this was not to be.

It was not a good race for Jaguar that year. First the cars had misfiring problems which were found to be caused by blocked filters. Once under way again, the car driven by Stirling Moss and Peter Walker lost its brakes, forcing it to retire. Not long after, the D-Type of Wharton and Whitehead dumped its gears, so that too was forced into premature retirement. Only the Duncan Hamilton, Tony Rolt car was left running and run it did. Even in the heavy rain that hit the race, Duncan was able to hammer along at speeds not deemed possible in such condition a few years earlier. More often than not, Hamilton was exceeding 170 mph, yet the leading car, a 4.9-liter Ferrari driven by Gonzales, could not be passed. At one stage in the race the Ferrari suffered a seven-minute pit stop and the Jaguar narrowed the gap to one and a half minutes. Once the track had dried out, however, the Ferrari took full advantage of its power superiority to lengthen the lead to two miles. An exciting race, well run by Gonzales and his winning Ferrari.

The D-Types were at Rheims for the 12 hour event there. They took revenge on the Ferraris, unable to keep up with the furious pace, and came in first and second. The third car, driven by Moss, retired.

As was stated earlier, the C- and D-Types were built to compete at Le Mans and in 1955 the Ds were back again,

this time with 7.5-inch longer noses. These were lengthened to take full advantage of the cars' aerodynamic shape. Another great British driver, Mike Hawthorn, had left Ferrari to race for Jaguar. Not only the Jaguars, but the Mercedes and Ferraris too, were very fast. In fact, the lap record was broken no less than ten times in the first two hours; first Fangio in the Mercedes, then Hawthorn in the Jaguar, then Castelotti in his Ferrari. Back and forth went the record until finally the Ferrari collapsed and retired. The Mercedes backed off, leaving the record in Hawthorn's hands. Real boys' adventure tales, this. Like the heroes featured in the British *Champion* stories, Mike Hawthorn was tall, handsome, blond and dashing. He went to the right schools and was just the sort of stuff English boys' heroes were made of, in those far-off, innocent days. Gritting his perfectly formed teeth – English comic heroes always gritted their perfectly formed teeth – Hawthorn was determined to trounce the German and Italian cars. He would show them what stern stuff British cars were made of. And show them he did.

Le Mans 1955 was marred by the dreadful accident that killed 80 spectators and injured 100 more. Pierre Levegh, driving for Mercedes, was racing side by side with two other cars when all three collided at 125 mph. The Mercedes on the inside track lost control and powered into the crowd, disintegrating and catching fire as it did so. So appalled was Mercedes that the entire team was withdrawn as a mark of respect. Later that year Mercedes announced its retirement from racing, and it was only in the late 1980s that the world's oldest car maker returned to do battle once more on the tracks of the world.

At the time of Mercedes' withdrawal, the 300SLR driven by Moss and Fangio was enjoying a two-lap lead, and it is likely that Mercedes would have won had it not been for the awful tragedy. Surprisingly, the French organizer continued the race, but with Mercedes gone, the Ferraris

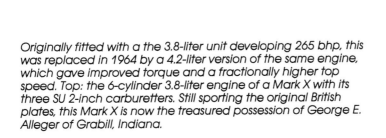

Originally fitted with a the 3.8-liter unit developing 265 bhp, this was replaced in 1964 by a 4.2-liter version of the same engine, which gave improved torque and a fractionally higher top speed. Top: the 6-cylinder 3.8-liter engine of a Mark X with its three SU 2-inch carburetters. Still sporting the original British plates, this Mark X is now the treasured possession of George E. Alleger of Grabill, Indiana.

SPECIFICATION
1963 XKE ROADSTER
SERIES I 3·8 LITER

Engine: 3781cc. Cylinder head: Straight port. Bore and stroke: 87 x 106mm. Max. power: 265bhp at 5500rpm. Max. torque: 260lb/ft at 4000rpm. Compression ratio: 9:1 (8:1 optional). Carburetion: 3 x 2in. SU HD8.

Chassis: Front suspension: independent wishbone, torsion bars, anti-roll bar. Rear suspension: independent lower wishbone, upper driveshaft link, radius arms, coil springs, anti-roll bar. Brakes: Dunlop discs, vacuum servo.

Measurements: Weight: 24cwt. Tires and wheels: Dunlop 6·40 x 15 RS5 on 15in. x 5K wire wheels. Track: 4ft. 2in. front and rear. Wheelbase: 8ft. Overall length: 14ft. 7·5in. Overall width: 5ft. 4·25in. Overall height: 3ft. 11in. (hood up). Maximum speed: 149·1mph. Fuel consumption: 19·7mpg.

When it first appeared in 1961 the E-Type, known in the USA as the XKE, was a sensation. It was still a sensation in 1963 when this Roadster (these and previous pages) was built. From its flush covered headlights to its exciting lines, the E-Type is everything a sportscar should be.

Photographed in the magnificent Papago Park, Phoenix, Arizona, the Jaguar looks as predatory as its name suggest. In 1963, the 3.8-liter DOHC engine (facing page top) made the E-Type one of the fastest cars available. Even today, more than thirty years after it was first launched, the E-Type's 149-mph top speed, and 0-60 time of 7 seconds, sounds truly astounding.

retired and two of the three D-Types out, it was not much of a victory for the lone Jaguar driven by Hawthorn and Ivor Bueb.

Within minutes of the start of the 1956 Le Mans 24-Hour Race, two Jaguars crashed, leaving only the intrepid Hawthorn/Bueb team to keep going for a further 23 hours and 55 minutes! Their car had problems which required several pit stops before the cause was traced to a cracked fuel line. By the time the car was repaired, they had fallen back to twentieth position; again the British pair kept going, but only managed to work back up to sixth place. There was disappointment in the Jaguar camp, but they had reckoned without Ecurie Ecosse.

Ecurie Ecosse was founded in Scotland by a former driver, David Murray, and car mechanic "Wilkie" Wilson. It was their idea to form a car-racing team to compete all over the world.

The first drivers were Ian Stewart, Bill Dobson and Sir James Scott-Douglas. All three shared one thing in common; they all owned Jaguar XK 120 cars. They were happy to join the new, all-Scottish racing team which began in earnest in 1952. They were too new to go international racing, so most of the first year was taken up with club events, in which Ecurie Ecosse chalked up ten firsts, six seconds and six third places.

In 1953 Ecurie equipped its racing fleet with three C-Types and raced them in three European events. It wasn't long before Ecurie's racing prowess came to the notice of

Jaguar, who sold them three disc-braked C-Types. By then Bill Dobson had left and was replaced by Ninian Sanderson and Jackie Stewart's older brother, Jimmy Stewart also joined the team. Ecurie entered seventeen events in 1954 and won an astounding twelve of them with C-Types, impressing Jaguar enough to sell the team three D-Types. More wins followed and soon the world began to notice, especially after Le Mans in 1956.

Even though Jaguar had its works team with its big name drivers and there were formidable works car entered like Ferrari and other world famous drivers to contend with, Ecurie entered a lone D-Type driven by Sanderson and another Ecurie signing, Ron Flockhart. Ecurie's entry was tongue-in-cheek, just to see what the race was like, testing whether it would be worth entering a full team in 1957. Winning the race might be nice, but nobody paid any attention to the little team from Scotland.

Le Mans is a brutal race, very cruel to engines, brakes and tires. And drivers. Retirements are commonplace, and those that run the whole twenty-four hours receive a hero's welcome from press and public alike. Any car that runs the distance virtually guarantees increased sales – not that the latter mattered much to Ecurie Ecosse; the team just liked winning. And win it did at Le Mans in 1956. The lone entry driven with determination by Sanderson and Flockhart came home first, thereby maintaining Jaguar's reputation. The winning car, however, was a strictly private entry running against the might of the works team – a David and Goliath situation, if you will.

Ecurie's fantastic win encouraged them to return in 1957, this time with a full team, but their further encouragement at the news that a works Jaguar team would not be entering was modified by the announcement that Jaguar was to pull out of racing. The decision was made in October 1956, and although the intention was

SPECIFICATION 1966 XKE SERIES I ROADSTER 4·2 LITER

Engine: 4235cc. Cylinder head: straight port. Bore and stroke: 92·07 x 106mm. Max. power: 265bhp at 5400rpm. Max. torque: 2383lb/ft at 4000rpm. Compression ratio: 9:1. Carburetion: 3 x 2in. SU HD8.

Chassis: Front suspension: independent, wishbone, torsion bars, anti-roll bar. Rear suspension: independent, lower wishbone, upper drive shaft link, radius arms, coil springs, anti-roll bar. Brakes: Dunlop discs with vacuum servo.

Measurements: Weight: 27·7cwt. Tires and wheels: SR41 185 x 15in. Track: 4ft 2·25in. front and rear. Wheelbase: 8ft 9in. Overall length: 15ft 4·5in. Overall width: 5ft 4in. Overall height: 4ft 2·5in. Maximum speed: 136·2mph. Fuel consumption: 18·3mpg.

Top: as the shot of this E-Type trunk shows, the car was never intended to carry large amounts of luggage. The original brochures, manuals and toolkit add interest to this superb 4.2-liter Roadster. Triple wipers and covered headlights identify this as a Series I.

that it should be temporary, it turned out to be one of the longest temporary retirements ever known; over thirty years would pass before Jaguar once again ventured on to the racetrack.

Everybody's eyes were on the little team from Scotland as the trio of D-Types assembled for the Le Mans traditional start. Sporting Scottish colors, the three cars hurtled along at breakneck pace. It wasn't all roses, of course, and the Jaguars had their problems. But it was Ecurie Ecosse who crossed the finishing line in first and second places, making it D-Types three years in a row and five Le Mans wins altogether for Jaguar during the fifties. As for Ecurie Ecosse, winner of two of the Le Mans races, the team continued racing successfully for a few years more before bowing gracefully and honorably from the scene.

D-Types were built between 1954 and 1956. All told seventy-one were made, which includes five that were destroyed in a factory fire. Production versions sold to private club teams and those with the money, accounted for most of the cars which were priced at £3,878 (about $8,000 at the 1955 rate of exchange). Relatively expensive then, D-Types today command astronomical prices, which is hardly surprising. After all, it was one of the most beautiful racing cars ever made, perhaps the most beautiful.

Which brings us back to the production cars. Taking several modifications done to the racing engines, Jaguar incorporated them in the engine of the new XK 140, introduced at the October 1954 London Earls Court Motor Show. Cubic capacity was the same as the XK 120, at 3442,

but brake horsepower was 190; but at 11 seconds 0-60 was slower than the XK 140's racing cousins. Top speed, however, was almost 130 mph, so the car was definitely no slouch and still held the title of fastest production car in the world.

As for the rest of the car, outwardly it had changed very little. It had massive American-style bumpers fitted front and rear and the grille was given seven thicker horizontal bars – the XK 120 had almost double that number but they were much thinner. In addition, a thin chrome strip ran down the middle of the hood, from the base of the windshield to the top of the grille, added, no doubt, in deference to American tastes. Rack and pinion steering replaced the Burman recirculating ball, worm and nut system. Borg-Warner's automatic was offered later in the run; the suspension was tougher and the hydraulic drum brakes were better.

In 1955 a more powerful XK 140 was announced. This was the XK 140MC, which was powered by the 210 bhp C-Type engine. It was able to go from rest to sixty in eight seconds and top speed was between five and ten mph faster than the normal 140. In the little over two years that the 140 was in production, almost 9,000 examples of the three body styles were produced. Apart from the heavy-handed bumpers and over-large chrome tail-lights that looked more like an afterthought, the XK 140 was every bit as beautiful as its 120 predecessor. Whether the same could be said of its successor is debatable, but that will be discussed later.

Between 1954 and 1957 quite a few events aided and

abetted Jaguar's fortunes. Le Mans was won three times, and the XK 140 introduced, but so was an all-new Jaguar, the compact 2.4 sedan. Viewed from the front, the 2.4 displayed its obvious lineage with aplomb and the car was not unlike the XK 150 in design.

The idea of a smaller sedan to cope with some of Europe's narrow, twisty roads, one that was more economical to buy, insure and run had been considered for a number of years. Originally a Jaguar sedan powered by four cylinders instead of six had been mooted. This idea, after numerous tests, was shelved, partly because the engine could not be made smooth or quiet enough for those used to Jaguar's traditional luxury. To solve the problem, a 2.4 liter version of the famous XK engine was eventually tried, and this successfully reduced the noise and vibration.

A departure for Jaguar was the use of unitary construction, a technique which company engineers had experimented with during the war. When the 2.4 was proposed, unitary construction was suggested the best way to build it. A lot of work needed to be done before the car was satisfactory enough for production and much of the development was carried out by Bob Knight, an engineer who eventually became Managing Director of Jaguar.

Knight was able to isolate the unit body with extensive use of various types of rubber and therefore rid the car of unwelcome vibrations and drumming. Both front and rear sub-frames were rubber mounted and supported the

By the time this E-Type was built in 1966 the XK engine (facing page bottom) had been in service some eighteen years. Constantly modified and improved, however, it was now rated at 265 bhp, propelling the car to a heart-stopping 150 mph. With the introduction of the 4.2 engine into the E-Type came other refinements, such as an all-synchromesh gearbox and improved brakes. The interior (top) was also updated, with new seating and redesigned dash.

conventional front independent, rear live axle, suspension layout. The result was an extremely quiet, maneuverable automobile with a power output of 112 bhp and a little over 100 mph top speed. Interiors were top grade leather and the refined car smacked of the elegance to which Jaguar owners had become accustomed.

Between 1955 and 1959, 19,400 2.4-liter Jaguars were produced, most of them ending up on the home market. Because sales of the XKs and Mark VII models had been so good in America, it was assumed that the 2.4 would do as well in the New World. It didn't, and although quite a few ended up in Canada, Americans themselves wanted big, brassy cars.

Big models did fairly well in America, though not as well as the XKs, combining a mid-Atlantic blend of refinement and *nouveau riche* vulgarity. They did exceptionally well in Britain, too, once restriction had been lifted; but Jaguars, especially the Mark VII to the Mark X, were always portrayed in films and on TV as the cars the wide boys, the shysters, would drive. The pre-war description of the Jaguar being a "poor man's Bentley" was hard to shake.

October 1956 served as the date for a new updated model. Now it was the Mark VIII succeeding the Mark VII, though its exterior differences were confined to a one-piece curved windshield in place of the old split-screen arrangement, two-tone paint (optional), and a slash of stainless trim adorning the sides – which didn't look unlike the leaping jaguar hood ornament in profile. Whether that was intentional or not, I don't know.

Other changes included a more luxurious interior, but the most newsworthy change took place under the hood. The XK engine, the 3442cc unit, is not measured by cubic capacity, rather by cubic inches, in America. Therefore this particular engine displaced 210 cubic inches and was rated at 210 bhp. Remember Chevrolet making a big thing about its 238/283? Well, here was Jaguar with one horsepower per cubic inch and nobody mentioned it. DeSoto also had an engine of one horsepower per cubic inch in 1957 and forgot to mention it as well. Really, this one hp per cid is of no real consequence because the way measurements were conducted in England were quite different from those of Europe and those of Europe different from America. Britain and Europe both share the metric system now, so they are the same, but America is still out on its own. It is more than frustrating that a single system of measurement is not yet universal.

The international political situation impinged upon the motorists of Britain at the close of 1956, when the Suez crisis resulted in gasoline rationing – a crippling ten gallons a month. This limit was felt severely by owners of thirsty cars, and the Jaguar Mark VIII tanks remained ruefully dry for many days each month.

It was March 1957 when the next new model arrived. This was the 3.4, a larger-engined version of the compact

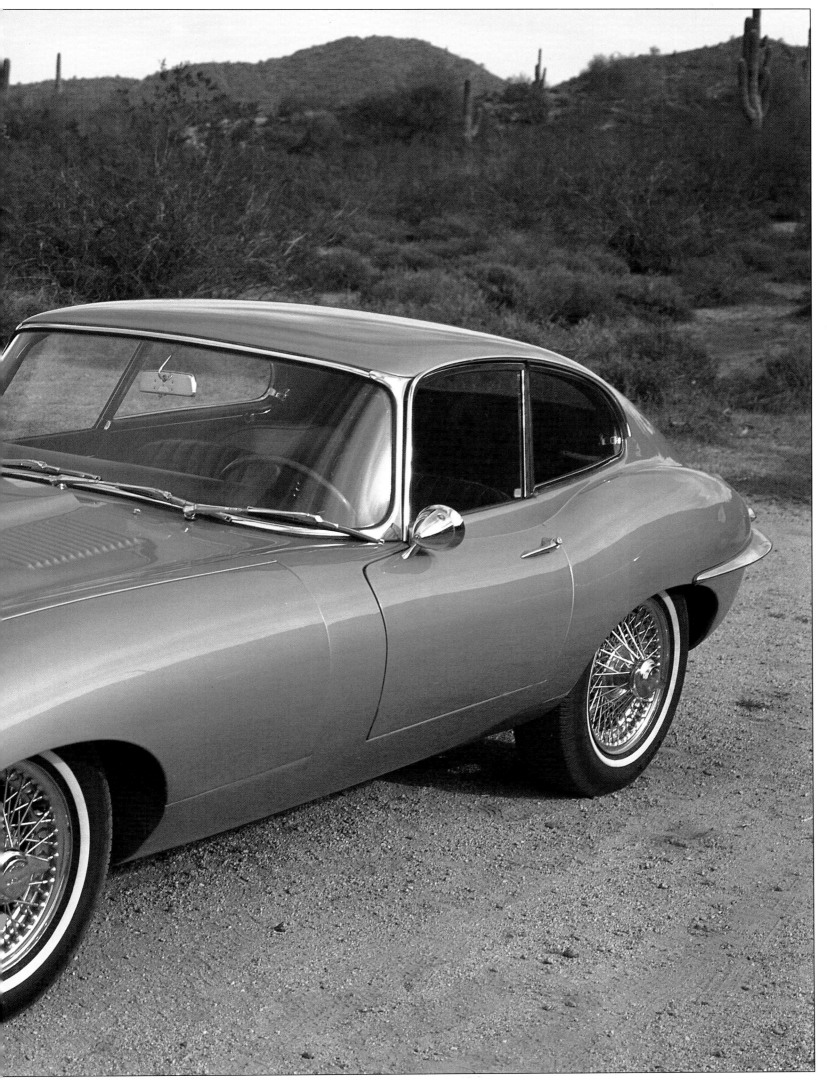

2.4, the same engine as in the Mark VIII (in America the 210/210).

Jaguar turned out 17,340 in the two years it was made. There were under-the-skin differences between it and its smaller sister, such as stiffer suspension, a new rear axle with modified Panhard rod and additional strengthening, all to cope with the larger engine. It was quite quick, certainly: able to reach over 120 mph and go to 60 in 9 seconds. Small wonder Jaguar sold so many in such as short time; at a mere £1,672 the 3.4 was tremendous value for money.

As Mercedes preferred the Frankfurt Motor Show for its new car announcements, so Jaguar favored the October Earls Court Show in London, (now transferred to an exhibition complex in the Midlands city of Birmingham). It was at the 1958 Earls Court event that Jaguar unveiled the Mark IX.

This was to be the final model of a body style that had been introduced in 1950 and outwardly little had changed. Over the years, chrome had been heaped on the car, though not with the same abandon stylists exerted when they plastered it all over the hapless 1958 Oldsmobile. The radiator grille was larger and framed in a generous band of chrome which more than suited the elegant frontal display. The eleven-year-old XK DOHC six was bored out to 3.8 liters and developed 220 bhp, and the 115 mph plus top speed could be brought down to sensible levels with the all disc-brake set-up which replaced the previous drums. Naturally the discs were standard as was the power steering. For all the creature comforts, leather upholstery, sun roof, a complete set of hand tools in the ample trunk, and better than average finish, the £1,995 (about $5,000 in 1959) the car cost was a bargain.

We have reached the end of a decade that was very special. Certainly, there were problems enough, but overall it was a memorable ten years. Before moving on into another decade, let us pause in order to look over the last of the legendary XK line, the 150.

Jaguar suffered a serious incident in February 1957 when its Browns Lane plant caught fire. Fortunately the blaze was swiftly brought under control before too much damage was done, but it resulted in the complete destruction of the jigs and several cars known as the XKSS. Only sixteen of these units left the factory before the blaze. The XKSS was a civilized version of the racing D-Type; Jaguar had found it possessed a lot of spare D-Type bodies that nobody wanted, so the 250-bhp XKSS was built. Its similarity to the E-Type was considerable and its maximum 150 mph speed the same. It would be very interesting to locate one of these priceless cars, which are no doubt zealously guarded by their owners. Lest we forget, the XK 150 débuted in May 1957.

It was fatter, heavier looking. The last of the XK series, the 150 was designed with America very much in mind. Hence the one piece curved windshield, slab sides without the pronounced dip that was almost a trademark, a wider grille and bumpers that looked as though they had fallen off a 1952 Chevrolet. And besides the car looking heavier, it was heavier, though the familiar DOHC engine was able to cope with that. Power disc brakes at each wheel was a production first for Jaguar and another instance why racing is good for the breed. Remember, Jaguar used discs on its racing cars first!

Like the other XKs the 150 came in three separate body

Few cars can match the E-Type for style, and the Coupé version (previous pages and right) is perhaps the most attractive of the body variants. It also happens to be the fastest, the 4.2-liter model being capable of 150 mph.

styles; coupé and drophead (convertible) at first, and a year later the roadster. Jaguar also offered several versions of the twin-cam six beginning with the base 190 bhp engine, with 210 and 220 bhp versions also available; the three had twin SU carburetors, and compression ratios of 7.0, 8.0 and 9.0 respectively. Another version was added in 1958. This was the XK 150S, which was powered by the same engine but used three large SUs, a different cam and a straight port head as the cylinder heads, once worked on by Harry Weslake, came to be known. In this form the engine developed a mean 250 bhp, but a year later Jaguar dropped the 3.8 liter engine into an XK 150S. This again had the three SUs and Harry Weslake's modifications. The engine developed 265 bhp and had a top speed approaching 140 mph and 0-60 was whipped up in 7.0 seconds. Shortly the larger engine was available in different states of tune, ranging from 220 bhp to the aforementioned 265.

With the various engine choices, the XK 150 should have sold more than the 7,900 of all versions marketed between 1957 and 1961. After all, the XK 120 went to 12,000 units, the XK 140 to 8,900 built. Production life for each model was six years for the 120, the 140 only for two, and the 150 lasted four years. Taking the number of years each model was produced shows the 140 as being by far the most popular of the XK series.

The new decade of the sixties was celebrated by the launch of new models and a remarkable new engine to come. William Lyons was honored by Queen Elizabeth II with a knighthood in recognition of his services to the country as a major dollar earner. But for the firm the new decade proved to be a very mixed bag of fortunes, many of which would cost the company dear as time went on.

SPECIFICATION
1966 XKE SERIES I
COUPE 4·2 LITER

Engine: 4235cc. Cylinder head: Straight port. Bore and stroke: 92·07 x 106mm. Max. power: 265bhp at 5400rpm. Max. torque: 283lb/ft at 4000rpm. Compression ratio: 9:1 (8:1 optional). Carburetion: 3 x 2in SU HD8.
Chassis: Front suspension: independent, wishbone, torsion bar, anti-roll bar. Rear suspension: independent lower wishbone, upper driveshaft link, radius arms, coil springs, anti-roll bar. Brakes: Dunlop discs, vacuum servo.
Measurements: Weight: 25·1cwt Tires and wheels: Dunlop 6·40 x 16 RS5; wheels as for 3·8 car. Track: front and rear 4ft 2in. Wheelbase: 8ft. Overall length: 14ft 7in. Overall width: 5ft 6in. Overall height: 4ft 0·25in. Maximum speed: 150mph. Fuel consumption: 18·5mpg.

Although conditions for driver and passenger were as cramped in the Coupé as in the Roadster, the former, with its sloping roofline and side-hinged tailgate, offered greater luggage space.

CHAPTER FOUR
THE E-TYPE AND THE DAY LORD STOKES CAME TO TEA

At the last Earls Court Motor Show of the fifties, Jaguar announced the Mark II. This was the compact replacement for the 2.4 and 3.4 models that first appeared four years earlier. Visually the car looked much the same at first glance; then the differences became apparent. Slimmer windshield pillars, a larger rear window, a narrower, more attractive grille with a thicker center bar and the circular grilles flanking the main one were replaced by spotlights. A new dashboard grouped the instruments in front of the driver, rather than in a central cluster as before.

As with other Jaguars, a choice of engine sizes was available, again versions of the same DOHC six. There was the 120 bhp 2.4 liter followed by the 210 bhp 3.4 and finally the 3.8 liter engine developing 220 bhp. Claims of 125 mph were not exaggerated; the Mark II was capable of a probable 130. In the little over seven years the Mark II was in production, Jaguar produced 83,000 units, the most popular being the 3.8 version – over 30,000 were built.

In this first year of the sixties, Jaguar, needing more space, bought out Daimler, inheriting a fairly diverse range of products. Daimler was Britain's oldest car company, having begun in 1893 by selling Daimler engines that were produced in Germany. That led to cars, a long-standing association with the Royal Family, many fine vehicles, including trucks, right up to the Daimler limousines and V8-powered SP 250 sports car, all part of the deal that Jaguar acquired. Shamefully, as time went on, Daimler lost its individual character to become a badge-engineered Jaguar.

While all this excitement was occupying the pages of the motoring press, the back-room boys at Browns Lane were putting the final touches to a pair of new cars that would rock the motoring establishment to its foundations. The first of these was not announced at Earls Court but at the Motor Show to end all Motor Shows, the one held at Geneva. Here, on a special stand in March 1961, was unveiled the Jaguar E-Type, which aroused the avid interest of the motoring world. It was the star, the sensation of the show, the culmination of five years gestation. As the world's motoring scribes tumbled over one another to take another incredulous look at the most sensuous four-wheeled feline ever to purr upon a Motor Show's boards, Sir William Lyons, Bill Heynes, designer Malcolm Sayer probably smiled quietly to themselves in the realization that they had another hit on their hands.

Apart from the engine and gearbox, the E-Type was all new. So new that it made every other sports car, including Ferrari, look old hat. Its origins were obvious; the ghost of the D-Type wouldn't lay down. If the body bore striking similarities, nothing else did. No Jaguar shared what was under the lithe skin of this beautiful cat.

The E-Type had a long, long hood, glass-covered headlights fitted flush into the fenders, a small oval opening at the front, split by a thin chrome bar supporting a circular

Eight inches longer and two inches higher, the 2+2 (these and previous pages) was Jaguar's answer to the motorist who wanted extra passenger or luggage capacity. The increase in size also meant greater comfort and easier accessibility through the enlarged doors, although the car's increased weight meant reduced performance.

SPECIFICATION
1967 XKE SERIES I 2+2
4·2 LITER

Engine: 4235cc. Cylinder head straight port. Bore and stroke: 92·07 x 106mm. Max. power: 265bhp at 5400rpm. Max. torque: 283lb/ft at 4000rpm. Compression ratio: 9:1. Carburetion: 3 x 2in SU HD8.
Chassis: Front suspension: independent, wishbone, torsion bars, anti-roll bar. Rear suspension: independent lower wishbone, upper driveshaft link, radius arms, coil springs, anti-roll bar. Brakes: Dunlop discs with vacuum servo.
Measurements: Weight: 27.7cwt. Tires and wheels: SP41 185-15in; wheels as for 3·8 car. Track: front and rear 4ft 2·25in. Wheelbase: 8ft 9in. Overall length: 15ft 4·5in. Overall width: 5ft 4in. Overall height: 4ft 2·5in. Maximum speed: 136·2mph. Fuel consumption: 18·3mpg.

Introduced in 1966, the E-Type 2+2 had its eye firmly fixed on the North American market, offering customers the option of automatic transmission. Both the Roadster and the two-seater Coupé remained in production alongside their long-wheelbase young brother.

badge in the center. Thin bumpers, like cat's whiskers, flanked each side of the oval. A sexy bulge graced the top of the hood, ending at the windshield as a rather narrow air intake. Center-lock wire wheels, a curved windshield fuselage sides that flowed softly into the curved rear and a pair of odd-looking tail-lights that were somehow out of place on an otherwise perfect design.

Under that long hood which, like the D-Type and the modern Corvette, was the entire front end and opened forward to reveal all, sat the 3.8-liter twin-cam six. Like the XK 150S, this particular engine developed 265 bhp and was good enough to take the E-Type up to 150 mph flat out. That was with standard 3.31:1 axle ratio; with the

optional 2.94:1 ratio probably around 170 mph would have been achieved.

A multi-tubular front frame combined with a monocoque center section was the main structure. Front suspension was torsion bars and wishbones and was fairly similar to the XK 150s. Steering was by rack and pinion and was extremely fast. At the rear, for the first time on a Jaguar, independent suspension. A large, pressed steel crossmember carried coil spring/shock absorber units, two to each side, which supported the rear wheels, the wheel uprights being located by transverse lower links and longitudinal radius rods. Anti roll bars, front and rear, made up the specifications.

Weighing in at 2,720 lb, the E-Type had a 96 inch

wheelbase and a driver/passenger compartment which some complained of as being too small, for like most sports cars, being built in the tradition of racing cars which are made to save as much space as possible, it was not easy to enter or exit. Its high, wide sills, little room between the steering wheel and seat, and low roof line, made it inconvenient for men of even average height; women wearing tight skirts and high heels had to wriggle!

Certainly it was not a car for the overweight or basket ball players, but if you can get into a ZR-1 then you will be able to get into the E-Type. If you cannot enter a ZR-1, then forget it! Only a Lincoln Town-Car limousine would do for you! Joking aside, sports cars have always been on the

SPECIFICATION
1972 XKE SERIES III
ROADSTER

Engine: 5343cc. Cylinder head: sohc, flat-head. Bore and stroke: 90 x 70mm. Max. power: 272bhp at 5850rpm. Max. torque: 304lb/ft at 3600rpm. Compression ratio: 9:1. Carburetion: 4 x Zenith 175CDSE.
Chassis: Front suspension: independent wishbone, torsion bars, anti-roll bar. Rear suspension: independent lower wishbone, upper driveshaft link, radius arms, coil springs, anti-roll bar. Brakes: Girling discs, vented front, servo assisted.
Measurements: Weight: 28·8cwt. Track: front 4ft 6·5in, rear 4ft 5in. Wheelbase: 8ft 9in. Overall length: 15ft 4in. Overall width: 4ft 1in. Overall height: 4ft 3in. Maximum speed: 146mph. Fuel consumption: 14·5mpg.

tight side in the tradition of racing cars which are made to save as much space as possible.

On the inside were two bucket seats which were well formed, and a row of dials and switches were mounted in the center, just above the console. The shift was set into the console as was the parking brake lever, and the steering wheel had a genuine wood rim. Changing gear was a joy; the little shifter fell eagerly into the driver's hands, but wasn't quite as much fun as one was led to expect. There was no synchromesh on first, and the elderly transmission was rather slow, the synchro on the remaining three gears being not very precise. Once the driver got used to the vagaries of the transmission, however, everything else was almost perfect. The car had a 50/50 weight distribution, nearly neutral steering, a standard limited slip differential and suspension that was forgiving. For the £2,160 the E-Type cost when new ($5,595 in the U.S.), Jaguar had done it again, with a bargain basement price for a car that made its far costlier contemporaries look leaden by comparison. Young men liked it, older ones too. Sex oozed from the E-Type like no other car – the owner was guaranteed a line of girls to choose from if he arrived at a dance in an E-Type.

It didn't matter where the E-Type went, it was an immediate hit. Americans fell over themselves to buy the XKE, as it was known in the U.S. According to the Publications International's *Great Book of Sports Cars*, 15,500 3.8 liter (230 cid) E-Types were produced before a considerably revised model was introduced in 1964. There was no difference in looks; the shape was the same. Overall length, which was

Like any other manufacturer, Jaguar was sensitive to criticism and sought to ameliorate wherever possible. This resulted in a new, all-synchromesh transmission and a larger engine. By redesigning the block the 3.8 was enlarged to 4.2 liters (258.4 cid). This didn't make the XKE any faster; Jaguar's engineers' object was to increase the torque from 260 to 283 lb/ft, thereby enhancing its flexibility and

Although the E-Type had undergone various changes with the introduction of the Series II in 1968, Jaguar's big news came in 1971 with the announcement of the Series III. Gone was the two-seater Coupé option, the choice now being the Roadster and 2+2, both on the latter's long wheelbase. More remarkable however was the introduction of the SOHC V12 5.3-liter engine, which supplanted the old 4.2-liter unit. A heavier looking hood as well as revised radiator grille identifies this Roadster (these and previous pages) as a Series III.

performance in rush-hour traffic and road contortions like Los Angeles' spaghetti junctions.

Had the largest standard production car to be built by Jaguar, the Mark X, been launched at the same time as the E-Type, it probably would have been lost in the mêlée, so Jaguar wisely waited until the London Motor Show of October 1961 before announcing it. Public reaction was, well, muted, compared to the emotional outpourings that greeted the E-Type and other Jaguars before it.

Weighing a colossal 4,200 lb the Mark X stretched a massive 202 inches overall and sat on a wheelbase of 120 inches. This was inherited from the Mark IX, as was the 3.8-liter engine and the transmission. Sir William had become interested in unit construction since his success with the compact 2.4 to Mark II series, and wanted the new Mark X to be so built. Chrysler in America had been using this form of construction since 1959 and, as the Mark X had been designed with America in mind, Sir William wanted to be up with, or even ahead of, developments coming from Detroit.

Dashboard is typically Jaguar (top) and badging (left) leaves the observer in no doubt that this car has the 5.3-liter V12. From the rear, the quadruple exhaust provides further identification. Increased width is evident in the car (facing page), with flared wheel arches accommodating the fatter tires. The 2+2 was finally dropped in 1973, and the Roadster two years later.

He needn't have worried. When it came to engine configuration, suspension and brakes, the Mark X was years ahead of anything the Americans had. With the exception of the radical compact Corvair, no U.S.-built car had independent suspension all round and none had disc brakes. The Corvette had both by 1965 but no full-sized American had independent suspension, coupled with disc brakes until the mid-eighties. The Mark X would be dead and forgotten by then. But in 1961 the Mark X was a refined masterpiece at £2,256 ($6,317), its nearest technical equivalent being the Mercedes, which cost three times as much.

For all its bulk – and it had plenty – the Mark X was very fast and was able to travel at 120 mph with consummate ease. As always with the big Jags, the ride was quiet, the roomy interior spoiling passengers for anything else. Rear seat passengers had fold-down tables that could be used to work on the company balance sheets or to spread out the Harrods' hamper James picked up that morning! And if you had a liking for wood, the Mark X interior displayed it in abundance. Perhaps it is a good thing modern-day automobiles use plastic. If they all used wood the way the Mark X did, there would be few trees left standing in the British Isles.

Jaguar had high hopes for the Mark X, but were surprised and disappointed at the negative response the car received. In Britain the Mark IIs were consistently popular sellers, where their compact measurements suited British tastes far better. The Mark X was perceived as too cumbersome, too ornate and not quite the car to be seen in at Ascot. For Americans, the opposite was true: the Mark X was too conservative – unless you lived in Hyannisport or Princeton – and for the Flash Harries of the day, that wasn't good enough.

Only 13,382 Mark X models were produced between

1961 and 1964; in desperation Jaguar popped the 4.2-liter engine under the hood, hoping the additional flexibility would bring more custom. It didn't. Sales petered out at 5,137 units for the year. In 1966 Jaguar changed the name to 420G to bring it into line with the Mark II series consisting of the 240/240 and 420. These numbers, as I am sure you will have worked out already or previously knew, refer to the engine size each car used; thus a 3.4 liter car was suffixed 340. Sales for the 420G remained on a downward spiral and the car was dropped in 1970.

Besides the already popular convertible and coupé, Jaguar launched the controversial 2+2 E-Type in the spring of 1966. It rode on a nine-inch longer wheelbase and its overall length was increased by eight inches, the idea being to create a family XKE. The added inches allowed a pair of occasional seats to be squeezed behind the front buckets, and the extra two inches in height would, Jaguar hoped, encourage those who had dismissed the two seater sports to think again. Apart from the none-too-attractive roof line, additional seats and extra length, the car was identical to other E-Types. But Jaguar purists didn't like the 2+2; for one thing it wasn't as handsome as the coupé and convertible, and they didn't like the idea that Jaguar was compromising one of the world's most beautiful cars for the sake of extra sales. And besides, the car was offered with Borg-Warner's automatic transmission as an option – amounting in many people's opinion to sacrilege!

Another new model joined the already prolific range in September 1963. This was the S-Type sedan, a rather clever blending of the Mark II and Mark X models. From the front to the rear pillars the S-Type was pure Mark II (which the car essentially was) but the lengthened rear was stolen from the Mark X. Underneath, the car benefited from the Mark X's independent rear suspension and both the 3.4 and 3.8 engines were offered, in 210 and 220 bhp forms. Overall it

SPECIFICATION
1978 XJ 12L
(LONG WHEELBASE)

Engine: 5343cc. Cylinder head: two flat-face, aluminum alloy. Bore and stroke: 90 x 70mm. Max. power: 285bhp at 5750rpm. Max. torque: 294lb/ft at 3500rpm. Compression ratio: 9:1. Fuel injection
Chassis: Wheelbase: 9ft 4·75in. Length: 16ft 2·75in. Brakes: Girling disc, 11·18in. ventilated front, 10·38in rear.
Measurements: Maximum speed: 147mph. Fuel consumption: 13·2mpg.

To counter criticisms of insufficient rear legroom in the XJ6, Jaguar announced a long-wheelbase version at the 1972 Frankfurt Show. The car shown on these and previous pages is a 1978 Series II fuel-injected XJ12L. Black rubber bumpers (facing page) were a feature of models destined for the American market. While the car offered superlative ride, performance and comfort, the company's reputation was at the time being tarnished by a series of crippling strikes as well as poor standards of quality that were a feature of Jaguar's years under the British Leyland umbrella.

was a great car, possessing superior road holding to the by now rather antiquated Mark II series, but it didn't sell as many as Jaguar would have hoped; from 1964 to 1968 24,900 units were produced, the larger engined version accounting for a heftier portion of the sales.

During the early sixties, Sir William Lyons took a leaf out of Errett Lobban Cord's book and began empire building. He had already acquired Daimler, ostensibly to make use of its factory space, then he took over Britain's famous trucking company, Guy Motors, who were notable for the first six-wheeled double-decker bus and four-wheel brakes. The company was responsible for some excellent medium and large trucks as well as military vehicles. By the early sixties, Guy found itself in serious financial difficulties, thus allowing Jaguar to step in. Next in line was Coventry-Climax, a company founded in 1903. Always engine builders, C.-C. was best known for its racing engines, which powered many a Formula 1 champion to victory. When Sir William took the company over in 1963, he welcomed the return of Wally Hassan, a talented engineer who had left Jaguar to join C.-C. in 1950.

Henry Meadows is a famous name in British motoring lore. Specialists in engine building, Meadows was formed in 1919 and became famous for its engines that powered a host of legendary British cars such as Frazer-Nash, Lagonda, Invicta and others. Once acquired by Sir William, all these companies began to do well again. This rather pleasant state of affairs was unfortunately not to last, and it was Sir William himself who, without realising it, planted the first seed of the eventual destruction of the companies he took over, and almost sounded the death-knell of his own.

By the mid-sixties, Jaguar was beginning to look like a jigsaw puzzle. There were so many cars and so many variations of the same cars that it was hard to know what belonged to which and to where. Then there was the problem of what would happen to Jaguar when Sir William, now 65 years old, decided to retire or passed on. He had two daughters but had lost his only son, killed in an accident on his way to Le Mans in 1955. By 1966 Sir William had come to a momentous decision: he would merge Jaguar with the British Motor Corporation, at that time the largest car maker in the land and made up of Austin, Morris, M.G., Riley and Wolseley. Morris and M.G. had always been together but the others were independent companies who, for one reason or another, had pulled together to make B.M.C.

At the time of the merger Jaguar was testing a top secret new engine design that even insiders knew nothing about. Four men comprised the major team: Bill Heynes, Jaguar engineering stalwart, Claude Baily, Walt Hassan and Harry Mundy. Mundy was a colleague of Hassan's when they worked together at Climax and Hassan brought him into Jaguar. It was these four who designed the fabulous V-12.

New American legislation came into effect aimed at improving the safety standards and exhaust emissions of domestic and imported cars. By the time the XKE Series II was introduced in 1968 it had suffered considerably. It wasn't as fast, safety regulations had increased its weight and the flush glass covers over the headlights had been removed to make way for the headlamps to move forward, as decreed by the law. The engine now had two Zenith carburetors in place of the three SUs, and 40 bhp was lost along the way. Larger tail-lights and parking-lights were added, as were front and rear sidelights. In the two years the Series II was in production, 13,490 were built; obviously some motorists were not deterred by the changes.

Also introduced in 1968 was the fabulous new Jaguar

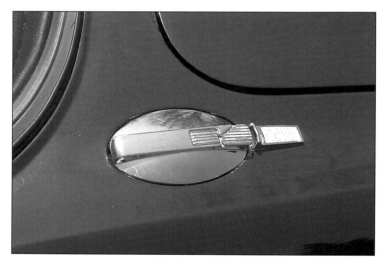

Luxury was stamped all over the XJ12L, the traditional leather and wood interior (top) cosseting driver and passengers. Distinctive alloy wheels (above right) add to the sporty nature of a five-seater saloon whose V12 engine (facing page bottom) gave it an astounding top speed of 147 mph, and 60 mph within 7.8 seconds. Attractive as the package was, however, many owners soon discovered the downside. This car had one problem after another, a common occurrence with most Jaguars built between 1972 and 1979. Happily, times have changed and Jaguar once again wears its badge with pride.

sedan. This was to be the answer to the critics' assertions that Jaguar was becoming top heavy at a sacrifice in quality. The new model, the XJ 6, would change all that. When it was announced, the S-Type disappeared and within two years Jaguar had stopped producing all the other sedans, concentrating solely on the E-Type, the XJ 6 and the XJ 6 variant, the badge-engineered Daimler Sovereign. Thinking of Daimler, most of which faded away after the Jaguar take-over, one car still carries on the old-world traditions that made the company famous. This is the Daimler Limousine, a hand-crafted car assembled in a separate corner of the Browns Lane factory by a special team of workers. Each car is an individual order, perhaps from royalty, a Middle East potentate or a large company.

It is hardly likely that any two Daimler Limousines are exactly alike. Of course they all share the same Mark X floor plan and the 4.2-liter version of the old twin-cam six (modern Jaguars use a different engine these days). This car is the last vestige of another age, when life was often more congenial, courteous and less threatened by excesses, so different in many way from the present – but that such cars as the Daimler Limousine can still be built is a reminder of what once was, and an example of what can be achieved.

Returning to the XJ 6, the car regarded by some as Sir William's ultimate achievement, work had begun on the design back in 1964. Everybody within Jaguar's top echelons knew that the time had come for a drastic pruning, but there had to be a car that would be capable of being all things to all men; sporty, comfortable, fast, not too large and not too small. The XJ was born.

September 1968 was the target date and, under the direction of Bill Heynes with Bob Knight working on ride and handling, the program was achieved in time. Sir William was closely involved with this, the last car created under his auspices. His mark can clearly be seen on the car, his creativity reliving better days, traditional characteristics … ignoring all this aerodynamic nonsense. This was a carriage in which to travel in style, not a racing car.

The wheelbase was 108.8 inches, in between the Mark II and Mark X. There were two versions of the venerable DOHC: a 2.8 liter for the car's domestic market where gasoline was expensive, and a 4.2 liter one for America. Interiors were all wood and leather with white-on-black instruments. Underneath, the suspension geometry had been altered slightly to give better anti-dive control on hard braking, four-wheel discs were featured all round and Dunlop had created new and wider low-profile tires for better all round drivability.

Up front the grille was the largest ever to grace a Jaguar sedan and was flanked by dual headlights, the larger pair in the fenders, two smaller ones mounted in-board and on the front of the hood. As for the rest of the car, it appeared to be a compromise of the models it was replacing, but no less attractive for that. The motoring press took the XJ 6 to heart and it was voted "Car of the Year" by British scribes. But dark clouds loomed on the horizon ….

Leyland was one of Britain's oldest commercial vehicle companies. This established and successful concern decided it had enough money to add further strings to its bow and started looking round for likely victims. It found Alvis and Rover first, and successfully trawled for Standard

Launched in 1975, at a time when Jaguar fortunes were at their lowest, the XJ-S (previous pages and right) came in where the legendary E-Types had left off. Even with the V12 under the hood, however, the XJ-S was no replacement for the E-Type.

SPECIFICATION
1983 XJS HE COUPE

Engine: 5343cc. Cylinder head: sohc, flat head. Bore and stroke: 90 x 70mm. Max. power: 285bhp DIN at 5500rpm. Max. torque: 294lb/ft at 3500rpm. Compression ratio: 9:1. Carburetion: Lucas electronic manifold fuel injection.

Chassis: Front suspension: independent wishbone, coil-springs, anti-dive anti-roll bar. Rear suspension: independent lower wishbone, upper drive shaft link, radius arm, coil spring, anti-roll bar. Brakes: Girling discs, ventilated front, servo assisted.

Measurements: Weight: 33·1cwt. Tires and wheels: Dunlop SP Super 205/70VR 15in x 6K alloy wheels. Track: front 4ft 10in, rear 4ft 10·5in. Wheelbase: 8ft 6in. Overall length: 15ft 11·5in. Overall width: 5ft 10·5in. Overall height: 4ft 1·5in. Maximum speed: 153mph. Fuel consumption: 12·8mpg.

Introduced in 1981, the XJ-S HE employed a high efficiency cylinder head that had been developed to improve fuel economy of the 12-cylinder 5.3-liter engine without adversely affecting performance. Clearly a disappointment to the many enthusiasts who had expected a sports car as a replacement for the much-loved E-Type, the XJ-S was nevertheless a very fast, luxurious machine. Capable of speeds in excess of 150 mph, it was not long before the newcomer began to show results on race tracks around the world.

SPECIFICATION
1986 XJS — C
CABRIOLET

Engine: 5345cc. Aluminum alloy cylinder head. 1 ohc per bank. Open deck aluminum block. Bore and stroke: 90 x 70mm. Max. power: 295bhp(DIN) at 5500rpm. Max. torque: (lb/ft DIN) 320 (433NM). Carburetion: Lucas/Bosch digital electronic fuel injection system.

Chassis: Front suspension: fully independent twin wishbones, coil springs and telescopic dampers. Anti-roll bar. Rear suspension: lower transverse wishbones, radius arms, twin coil springs and telescopic dampers. Steering: rack and pinion power assisted energy absorbing column with fore and aft adjustment. Brakes: servo assisted 4 wheel discs, ventilated at front. Transmission: 3 speed automatic torque converter.

Measurements: Weight: 1800Kg. Tires and wheels: 6·5J x 15. Starfish castalloys. 215/70 VR15 low profile steel belted radials. Wheelbase: 102·0in. Overall length: 187·6in. Overall width: 70·6in. Overall height: 49·7in. Ground clearance: 5·5in.

Triumph in 1961. Now Leyland had become a bona fide automobile manufacturer in its own right. Chief of Leyland was Sir Donald Stokes. No Sir William Lyons was he; cars were another means to an end, especially financial . By the mid-sixties Leyland had become the Great White Shark, ever searching for ailing motor corporations to capture. It found one, a very juicy morsel called British Motor Holdings – or B.M.C. to everyone else.

The reason that British Motor Corporation became British Motor Holdings was to allow B.M.C. and Jaguar to share a common board of directors but to operate quite separately from each other. This worked well for a couple of years, but B.M.C. found itself in dire financial difficulties mostly brought on by strikes and rationalization – perhaps over-rationalization! Whereas Jaguar hadn't rationalized enough, B.M.C. went overboard. Famed designer Alec Issigonis, creator of B.M.C.'s only decent money spinner the Mini, had designed the dreadful front wheel drive Austin-Morris-Wolseley-Riley series. All were identical with the exception of the front grilles, and I recall some wag writing to one of the motoring papers suggesting it might have been better if B.M.C. designed one body and supplied five different grilles for it. One would fit an Austin grille to go shopping; a Wolseley grille for the country club; the Riley one for the golf tournament and so on. The writer's letter may have been tinged with heavy sarcasm but it was an excellent idea all the same. Not that it would have made a lot of difference in 1968; few were buying the existing products and it is equally unlikely they would have bought a five-in-one car. Quite simply, B.M.C.'s products were ugly and workmanship was a thing of the past.

By contrast, Jaguar cars were beautiful cars and were selling well. After Sir William's spate of empire building, however, Jaguar resources were stretched and there was little it could do to help its ailing bedfellow. Attracted by the scent, the Great White Shark struck, and with one mighty gulp swallowed B.M.H. whole. Sir Donald Stokes must have been pleased as he sat down with British Motor

Now with vastly improved quality and better fuel economy, the XJ-S accounted for 25 percent of Jaguar production. A new model, the XJ-SC Cabriolet (previous pages and right) was announced in 1984, powered by the all-new AJ6 24-valve six-cylinder engine (the old DOHC six continued to power the large hand-built Daimler limousines). The model illustrated boasts the larger V12 engine.

In 1985 the V12 was fitted to the Cabriolet (top) thus giving it a 150-mph top speed. The interior (left) is lavish and well finished, while the typically smooth engine gives this big cat characteristics one has come to expect of Jaguar.

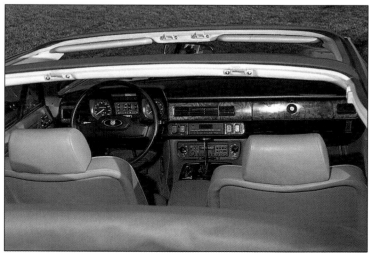

Holdings directors, but they were not at all happy with the situation in which they found themselves.

At the time of the take-over, Sir Donald and his advisers may have thought they were doing the British motor industry a great deal of good yet by 1968 there wasn't much left of it (Ford, Vauxhall and Rootes were all American owned), so the only sensible course was to merge with each other. As time would shortly tell, this was an improbable remedy, for no one had bothered to learn from similar protective merges in the U.S., such as Studebaker-Packard and Nash-Hudson; all these great names were gone within a dozen years.

Lord Stokes was very personable, very persuasive. He outlined his plans for the salvation of Britain's motor industry under his aegis. First the merged companies would trade under the name of British Leyland and the cars within the group would be split off into divisions, each division working independently of the other. There were doubters, but overall Stokes' plan met with approval. But Stokes and his invisible men, had forgotten about the workers, the men who put the cars together. And those workers had unions.

There was a total lack of communication between blue collar and white. It seemed that the shop floor was a no-man's-land for upper management. British Leyland was

travelling on a course parallel to Captain Bligh on The Bounty and mutiny was in the offing. So far Jaguar remained unaffected, for the honeymoon was not yet over, primarily because the invisible axe-men dare not touch Jaguar for the time being. To have done so would have caused a revolution. Six years later, Lord Stokes had many reasons to regret all that he had done and Jaguar was sorry that it ever allowed him to come to tea.

CHAPTER FIVE
INTO THE ABYSS AND BACK

Jaguar has always surprised and delighted, but never more than in March 1971, when it launched the Series III E-Type. There were external differences from the earlier series, but under the hood was a real surprise, a magnificent V-12 engine, the first British one since Daimler's Double-Six and the only one apart from Ferrari and Lamborghini. Since the Italian cars were specialists vehicles Jaguar's new engine was the first production V-12 since the Lincoln Continental unit was dropped in 1948.

So as not to compromise the E-Type's shape, not forgetting economics and simplicity, the V-12 was a single overhead cam unit rather than the DOHC design originally considered. It was a beautiful sight, a jewel that featured a 60 degree angle between the aluminum cylinder blocks (the cylinder heads and crankcase were aluminum as well) and each cylinder bank had a single overhead camshaft. A seven main bearing crankshaft, Lucas

electronic ignition and four two-bbl Zenith carburetors were other features.

Of course this engine would roll! Hardly surprising when you consider its cubic capacity was 5343 (326 cid) and it developed 272 bhp (DIN), 314 (SAE) at 6,200 rpm. In European tune, the V-12 was easily capable of 150 mph and 0-60 came up in about 6.5 seconds. American emission-laden versions would top 135 mph and it took 7 seconds to reach 60. This was pretty quick by any standards, especially in 1971 when American manufacturers were cutting back on performance.

As for the body, the lines had been spoilt. The open-mouthed front was replaced by a latticework grille. This was emphasized by an oval chrome frame flanked on each side by large overriders. To accept the larger engine, the 104-inch wheelbase of the 2+2 was used, enabling V-12 convertible owners to have the Borg-Warner automatic if they so chose. Vented front discs, power rack and pinion steering, wider track and tires and a 21.5-gallon gas tank, made up the world's cheapest V-12: £3,387 or $8,000 – this was a bargain-basement price for such a car when compared to the two Italian makes, but was $2,500 more than a V-8 Corvette. It was a shame about the front and rear of the new model. Although the overall shape was left alone, the heavy-handed redesign at the front did the car no favors; by 1974, with the addition of huge rubber block overriders in accordance with U.S. bumper laws, the E-Type looked even worse.

By 1975 the E-Type Experience was all over. In production for fourteen years, with 72,507 units built (15,300 of these were V-12s), the E-Type would be sadly missed. It was immensely affordable, and by the end still cost only half the asking price of a Dino 246GT or a Porsche 911. Plus it had V-12 power. What more could anyone want?

SPECIFICATION
1987 XJ6 SALOON

Engine: 2919cc. Cylinder head: alloy sohc. Bore and stroke: 91 x 74·8mm. Max. power: 155bhp at 5000rpm. Max.torque: 1763lb/ft at 4300rpm. Compression ratio: 12·6:1. Carburetion: Bosch electronic injection.
Chassis: Front suspension: independent, unequal length upper and lower wishbones, coil springs, anti-roll bar. Rear suspension: independent, lower wishbone/upper driveshaft link, radius arms, twin coil springs. Steering: rack and pinion, power assistance standard. Brakes: hydraulic power-assisted 4 wheel discs, ventilated at front.
Measurements: Weight: 3793lb. Maximum speed: 120mph.

A much redesigned and updated version of the superlative XJ6 appeared in 1987, replacing all Series III cars except for the long-wheelbase V12 HE and Daimler saloon. The culmination of a seven-year, £200 million development program, the new range continued Jaguar's remarkable tradition of quality and refinement. Power for the new cars came from the specially designed all-aluminum 2.9 and 3.6-liter AJ6 engines. This car is pictured outside the suitably regal Goodwood House.

Shortly after the first V-12 found its way into some happy owner's driveway, Jaguar used the engine in the XJ sedan. This was in 1972, and in deference to public criticism about the lack of rear leg room, the XJ-12 was given a longer wheelbase, stretched to 112 inches. The same was done with the 4.2-liter XJ-6 – both V-12 and the 4.2 liter carried the suffix "L" to denote long wheelbase – but the 2.8-liter model was left alone, possibly because it would be dropped from the line-up very shortly. The new XJs were known as Series II models, and announced at the same time was a stylish two-door hardtop coupé on the shorter, 108.8 inch wheelbase. This was the XJ-6C (for coupé) and XJ-12C. Both stayed in production three years before being killed

off as a result of the decision to drop the short wheelbase sedan.

An XJ-12 sedan cost around $11,000 in 1974, so prices were beginning to match other makes. This was unfortunate as Jaguar cars were suffering the worst bout of quality control and poor workmanship ever to affect a European car of stature. Ever since the 1968 Leyland take-over, problems had gone from bad to worse, with labor relations deteriorating to their lowest ebb in modern industry, for Lord Stokes and his management refused to listen.

Wolseley, Riley, Standard, Guy, Coventry Climax – all ruthlessly disposed of by the hatchet men. Because of B.L.'s antics, Morris and MG left the stage within a few years, and the strikes continued, more wage demands resulting because of Britain's runaway inflation (it reached a peak of 25 per cent by the late seventies), and Jaguar quality sank yet deeper.

All the old familiar faces at Jaguar were disappearing – fortunately due mostly to retirement. Arthur Whittaker and William Heynes both retired in 1968, Sir William Lyons, the founder, called it a day at the age of 70 in 1972. "Lofty" England became chairman but decided after a short time to relinquish the post and moved to Austria. Only Bob Knight and Wally Hassan remained of the old team. Malcolm Sayer, responsible for so much of Jaguar's beautiful designs, died of a heart attack in the seventies, but will be remembered as long as there are E-Types still surviving.

By early 1974 Lord Stokes was a worried man. He realized he had lost complete control over the amorphous mass he managed, and that actually he had destroyed more than he ever created. Oil crises hadn't helped, Jaguar sales were a trickle of what they once had been, and the company's financial situation was so desperate that the government, in its concern for British business and in order to keep the concern going, was forced to hand over £50,000,000.

In 1975 British Leyland was nationalized and the government commissioned Sir Donald Ryder to look after the company's affairs. His findings were published in the Ryder Report, which suggested centralization of all management and technical teams. Jaguar was extremely unhappy about this but there was nothing it could do.

While these extraordinary events were tearing the industry apart, Jaguar managed to launch the E-Type's successor, the vastly different XJ-S. Bob Knight, one of the few original Jaguar men with the company, was in control of its development. Because money was tight during the car's gestation period, it was agreed it would share as many components as possible. Ergo, the XJ-S inherited the short wheelbase XJ-6 floorpan, V-12 engine and sedan suspension. The result was an interesting blend of ideas – the rear pillars and backlight had their origins in the Dino 246GT while the rest of the car had a faint trace of Pontiac Trans-Am about it. A two-door coupé, the XJ-S was a grand tourer that would be just as at home cruising down Horse Guards Parade in London as driving through the Alps.

As cars go the XJ-S was a miracle machine. Reasonably priced, very refined, it could top 150 mph with ease (the V-12 engine developed 285 bhp), was comfortable, though not as comfortable as an XJ-6 due to its lack of space that was dictated by the style of the vehicle. I drove a couple of 1989 models, a coupé and the convertible; as road-going performance vehicles there is little to touch them. Of the two, the coupé is the most comfortable while the convertible, which is a two-seater, becomes a bit cramped on a long journey. Both cars have all the creature comforts, and the quality of finish in both is impeccable, the best I have seen on a Jaguar for a long time. However, the days of value for money have long gone; the convertible costing £41,200 and the six cylinder coupé £27,200.

Michael Edwardes was appointed head of B.L. and was knighted for his efforts in rescuing the beleaguered

These and previous pages: the 1988 version of the XJ6. Impeccable finish and the world's best ride are a far cry from a decade earlier. The new six-cylinder engine is a joy, whether in 2.9 or 3.6-liter form.

company. What he was unable to do was to reinstate Jaguar's sullied reputation. Since everything had been centralized, all Jaguar bodies were built by one of B.L.'s plants, whose workmanship standards left much to be desired. I remember America's first Formula One World Champion, Phil Hill, remarking how much he liked Jaguars, but that he had to switch to a Mercedes to gain reliability. Phil Hill campaigned in E-Types at Le Mans in the early sixties.

In 1980 Sir Michael appointed John Egan as Jaguar's new chairman. When Egan came in, he found a company in a precarious position, its production down to 14,000 units a year from a mid-seventies 30,000, and losing almost a million pounds a week. Bob Knight was now Managing Director and he had succeeded in putting together a decent team of Jaguar loyalists. On his retirement in 1980, Knight was offered control of the awful Castle Bromwich plant, the makers of Jaguar's lackluster bodies. He accepted and Egan took over.

Egan was ruthless. He saw the problems affecting the quality of Jaguar and set to work removing suppliers and threatening others with lost contracts if they didn't improve. He was equally ruthless with the Castle Bromwich plant. Slowly but surely Egan won respect and loyalty, culminating in greatly improved Jaguars, which resulted in increased sales. By 1984 the turn-around had been so complete that Liverpool Docks were lined with Jaguars waiting to be shipped to America and elsewhere.

New engines were introduced; the faithful six-cylinder unit had been in service since 1948 and was long overdue for replacement. That replacement finally arrived in 1984. Called the AJ-6 (for advanced Jaguar Six) the engine was first introduced in the XJ-S 3.6, the numerals attesting to this 24-valve engine's size, which was almost as fast as the updated V-12, at 145 mph. The V-12 was given new cylinder heads (developed by a Swiss engineer called Michael May) designed to have lean-burn characteristics and superior fuel economy. Named HE for High Efficiency, the engine powers Jaguars to this day.

Jaguar's fortunes had grown so much that Mrs. Thatcher's government announced that the company was to be returned to the private sector. Conservative governments dislike state-owned enterprises, so it was obvious they would dispose of this business as soon as the climate was viable. The company was floated on the stock market and there was a scramble for the shares being traded at about $3.00 each, resulting in ten times as many applications as there were shares. On the final morning, with a deadline of 10 am, there was great excitement in the City of London as people fought to buy shares. A furious day for the Stock Exchange but a thankful one for Jaguar, who found themselves once more a private concern.

Like Sir Michael Edwardes, John Egan became Sir John for his magnificent saving of Jaguar's name. In the year of his knighthood (1986) Jaguar announced the new XJ-6. A new model had been mooted for some time, the existing model being given facelifts to keep it fresh. Code-named XJ-40, the new car had to reflect old-world tradition with state-of-the-art computer technology. As can be seen from the design, the car was evolutionary rather than revolutionary and all the better for it.

Engines are a 2.9- and a 4.0-liter six, and the 5.3 liter V-

147

SPECIFICATION
1988 XJ6 SALOON

Engine: 3590cc. Cylinder head: alloy dohc. Bore and stroke: 91 x 92mm. Max. power: 165bhp at 5000rpm. Max. torque: 249lb/ft at 5000rpm. Compression ratio: 9·6:1. Carburetion: Lucas electronic injection.
Measurements: Weight: 3903lb.

New technology coupled with old-world craftsmanship accounts for the enthusiastic reception that met the new XJ6. Alloy wheels were now offered as standard on the top-of-the-range Sovereign and Daimler models, while the "base" versions were fitted with pressed steel wheels and elegant hub caps (above). The interior (top) is typically Jaguar, with a choice of wool fabric or leather upholstery and wood door cappings and fascia. As well as boasting two new power units, the cars were available either with five-speed manual transmission or the four-speed automatic featuring the new J-gate selector. All-round independent suspension provides superb ride, further enhanced by the optional ride levelling system on the rear suspension.

151

12HE. Besides the Jaguars, there are Daimler versions as well, which are exactly the same apart from Daimler's traditional fluted grille, both cars sharing a high degree of comfort, and stability second to none. As for design, this latest XJ-6 is by far the best looking of all, even if there is a hint of the 735 BMW about it. One thing is absolutely for sure; the Jaguar's degree of club-style comfort is vastly superior to the German car.

As Jaguar approached the nineties, it did so with excellent sales, a strong model range and an alarming drop in profits, due to the dollar's downward spiral in the money markets. Then, on 15 September 1989, the giant Ford company announced its intention to buy 15 per cent of the famous British car. The offer received a decidedly lukewarm response and Jaguar directors issued a statement to the press that Ford's offer was "unwelcome".

Ford's arch rival, General Motors, stepped on the scene with an offer Jaguar found hard to resist. If the deal went through, G.M. would want a minor investment in exchange for a sorely needed financial transfusion and Jaguar independence. Negotiations began, and even while the two sides were talking Ford was buying Jaguar shares. This forced up Jaguar's share price and it began to look as though there would be a war between the two giants for Jaguar, who must have felt terribly important in consequence.

In the meantime, the U.S. government gave permission to Ford to buy 15 per cent of Jaguar, the maximum allowable under the Articles of the company. Then, on 26 October, G.M., who had been very quiet, announced it was buying 15 per cent of Jaguar. On 31 October, Nicholas Ridley, the British government's Secretary of State for Trade and Industry, said the government had no objection if shareholders wanted to cancel the "Golden Share" issued when Jaguar became independent in 1984. The idea behind this "Golden Share" was that the government could protect Jaguar from any take-over bid until 31 December 1990. An Extraordinary General Meeting was held to ask the shareholders whether they would cancel their "Golden Shares". To allow a take-over bid in this manner required 75 per cent of the shareholders to agree, which they did, and the way was clear for a take-over.

Once Ford heard the decision it lost no time in offering to buy out Jaguar for £8.50 a share ($13.60). This represented $2.5 billion Ford was willing to pay for Jaguar. At the same time G.M. decided that it didn't really need Jaguar that badly and dropped out of the picture. Naturally Ford's offer was accepted and the 68-year-old company that hailed from Blackpool had been bought for a record price. Even Ford admitted after its purchase that it had paid too much, but it was "worth it".

Under the agreement Ford will allow Jaguar to remain a separate entity, have its own self-sustaining capital structure and its own Board of Directors. Jaguar's chairman would report to Ford of Europe's chairman and Ford would supply the necessary monies to help Jaguar development. At the same time Jaguar would have the advantage of Ford's worldwide engineering and manufacturing experience. In

Unveiled at the Geneva Motor Show in 1988, the XJ-S Convertible (previous pages and right) became the company's first fully open-top car since the death of the E-Type Roadster. Air conditioning, power-operated roof and anti-lock braking were standard features on this V12-powered car.

SPECIFICATION
1990 XJS CONVERTIBLE
V12

Engine: 5345cc. Cylinder head: aluminum alloy,sohc, flat head Bore and stroke: 90 x 70mm. Max. power: 285bhp at 5150rpm. Max torque: 310lb/ft at 2800rpm. Compression ratio: 11·5:1. Carburetion: Marelli electronic.

Chassis: Front suspension: independent, wishbone, coil springs, anti-roll bar. Rear suspension: independent, transverse lower wishbone, upper drive shaft link, radius arms, coil springs, anti-roll bar. Brakes: electronically controlled anti-lock, hydraulic assisted..

Measurements: Tires and wheels: Sports alloy 6·5 x 15in. with 235/50 VR15. Track: front 4ft 6·6in, rear 4ft 11·2in. Wheelbase: 8ft 8in. Overall length: 15ft 6in. Overall width: 6ft 1in. Overall height: 4ft 1·7in. Maximum speed: 145mph.

Alloy wheels in a spoked design grace this XJ-S Convertible. Long and low, the lines of the XJ-S benefit from the drophead treatment, while the fully lined and insulated power top, which can be raised in just 12 seconds, protects the occupants from the worst of the elements. Unlike many convertibles, the Jaguar offers a solid glass, tinted, heated rear window.

a forty-five-page document discussing the formal Offer to Purchase, Ford set out its proposals, thus:

"Ford has been exploring actively opportunities to develop its presence in the worldwide luxury car market. The acquisition of the Company by Ford represents an important step towards fulfilling this objective and will, at the same time, strengthen Ford's existing substantial commitment to the United Kingdom.

"Ford and the Company believe that there is considerable potential to increase sales volume for the Company's product range in Europe, the United States and other parts of the world. Over the longer term, Ford and the Company expect to enhance significantly the Company's prospects and presence throughout the world though the joint development of new product and manufacturing ideas.

"To continue to compete effectively in world markets, Ford and the Company believe that the Company will need greater resources than it currently has. Ford and the Company believe that Ford will bring the following strategic benefits:

"substantial financial resources which will enable the Company to accelerate new product developments, and

"access to a worldwide technology base. Ford and the Company believe that there are substantial benefits to be gained for both companies in building upon the Company's history as a manufacturer of fine sports and luxury cars."

On paper it looked good, but in reality, will it work and will Ford keep its word? Only time will tell. In the meantime Jaguar is producing some fine machinery including the XJR 4.0, the work of Jaguarsport, the company's official racing arm, run by Jaguar racing boss Tom Walkinshaw. As most readers probably know, Jaguar has been back in official racing for a number of years, with wins at Le Mans and Daytona to its credit. The XJR 4.0 is almost the same as the regular XJ-6 but with more spirited performance. But is £39,450 (about $63,000) worth paying for a few mph more? Jaguars are no longer the amazing value-for-money contenders they once were. The price mentioned is more than one would pay for a BMW 735i or a Mercedes 420SE. Autocar/Motor's road test pointed out that the £14,000 cheaper 2.7 liter Sterling can match the XJR's 0-60 in 8.3 seconds. Seems that something is not quite right here ....

Whatever the price, Jaguar is still a fine automobile, one of the best. A lot depends on what Ford does over the next few years, for it is doubtful whether Jaguar will maintain the independence it would like; Sir John Egan, the man who saved Jaguar, left as chairman in June 1990 and handed over to a Ford man, William J. Hayden. C.B.E. Born in East London, 61-year-old Hayden had the distinction of being the only non-American Ford vice-president, a company he has been with since 1950.

How will Jaguar develop in the next few years? As I write this, rumors circulating in England say Ford is about to axe Jaguar's pet F-Type project. The F-Type was to be a 400-horsepower, 200-mph sports car powered by a 4-liter six-cylinder engine. Development of this fantastic sounding automobile has often been put on the back burner because of lack of funds, but now the funds are there the F-Type may die, stillborn – or may have done so by the time the reader reached this page. It might have been saved, but it is doubtful. Ford's stated goal is for Jaguar to produce more, and insiders are saying Ford will probably develop a cheaper line of Jaguars to sell in the $20,000 to $30,000 range. Sir John Egan increased production from 14,000 units a year to 50,000 in 1989, but it is said Ford might like that to increase to 400,000 units a year.

That would be one way to get its $2.5 billion back ....

SPECIFICATION 1990 VANDEN PLAS 4·0 LITER SALOON

Engine: 4·0 liter 3780cc. Max. power: 223bhp at 4750rpm. Max. torque: 278lb/ft at 3650rpm. Compression ratio: 9·5:1. Carburetion: electronic fuel injection.
Chassis: Front and rear suspension: 4 wheel independent. Brakes: 4 wheel disc with ABS. Transmission: 4 speed automatic overdrive.
Measurements: Weight: 3960lb. Tires and wheels: alloy road wheels with Pirelli radial ply tires. Wheelbase: 113·0in. Overall length: 119·4in. Overall width: 79·3in. Overall height: 53·1in. Fuel capacity: 22·8 gals.

The epitome of luxurious motoring, the 1990 Vanden Plas (these and previous pages) boasts a 4-liter six, anti-lock brakes, and all the refinements that the discriminating driver might wish for. Square headlights (overleaf) distinguish the Vanden Plas, as well as Sovereign and Daimler models, from the base XJ6. With its high standard of finish and lively performance, the award-winning XJ6 range maintains Jaguar's strong claim for the title "Best Car in the World."